Dedication

To Mollie, my dear sister, who, as a little girl
asked me when I would open my heart to the
Lord Jesus, and to whom I have been, and still
am, so close

To Mary, my beloved wife, colleague, soul-mate,
and fellow-soldier in the ministry

To the memory of those who influenced me
most in my early years: my parents, Ivan and
Doris, Auntie Mackie, Uncle Ron, Rev Bernard
Johanson

To our beloved children, Colin, Heather and
Christine who, with their spouses, are carrying
the gospel to the next generation

To my esteemed co-workers in the battle for
souls—what times we had together in His
Presence and at His feet!

**Dr Colin Peckham as principal of
the Faith Mission Bible College**

25th July 1861	Fred and Elizabeth Peckham married in England
4th November 1861	Arrive in Durban, South Africa
1902	Bertie (Fred's son) married Fanny Franklin
30th November 1904	Ivan (Bertie's son) born
5th November 1927	Ivan married Doris Gladwin
20th June 1936	Colin Neil Peckham born
24th May 1951	Colin trusted Christ for salvation
1954 & 1955	Studies at Cedara Agricultural College, Natal
1958 & 1959	Glenvar, AEB Bible College, Cape Town
1960–1967	Evangelism throughout South Africa
1968 & 1969	Youth Work
12th April 1969	Married Mary Morrison of the Faith Mission, Scotland, Lived in Johannesburg
12th August 1970	Colin Morris born in Johannesburg
1st January 1971	Went to AEB Bible College as Lecturer (later principal)
4th August 1971	Heather Ann born in Cape Town
April–July 1972	Furlough in UK
29th April 1974	Christine Mary born in Cape Town
April–July 1976	Furlough in UK
July 1982	Emigrated to UK as principal of the Faith Mission Bible College, Edinburgh
June 1999	Relinquished the College after 17 years
July 2001	Retired to Broxburn near Edinburgh and to itinerant ministry in this and other countries
November 2009	Called home to Heaven

Commendations

From a happy, enjoyable childhood on a South African farm to evangelist, choir master, Bible teacher, editor, Bible College principal, author and international preacher, *Adventures of Faith* is an account of God's grace in salvation, God's guidance in service and God's goodness in supplying needs in remarkable ways. It tells of a life fully yielded to God, that has touched many of all ages and prepared them for service in God's harvest field and for eternity.

A wonderful record!

Rev Tom Shaw, BA MTh,
Congregational Minister and former President of the Faith Mission

In this fascinating life story, Dr Colin Peckham has given clear testimony to the reality of God's existence and presence. The heavenly Potter tenderly moulded one chosen out of the people; remaining with him, teaching and leading him to make him that very special instrument, meet for the Master's use! The writer proves that by maintaining a personal, intimate relationship with God, he is ever faithful to his promises and that he answers prayer—often in wonderful and mysterious ways!

The reader will be thrilled to learn of countless victories won in Christ's name. Colin has kept an amazingly careful record of his ministry as an evangelist and Bible teacher. The events, as God led him on, seem to flow as separate streamlets and to merge into a river of victory, praise and glory!

I trust that this thrilling story of a much-used servant of God will be read with as much blessing and delight, as it has proved to me! Your faith will be strengthened and your heart stirred, strangely warmed and filled with hope and joy as you read how God rewarded the wholehearted consecration of this young man, how he brought to him a wife with the same burden and vision, how he filled his heart with heavenly joy, with a passion for souls and with a consuming and lasting love for his Master!

Pieter Scholtz,
Former General Superintendent of the Africa Evangelistic Band, South Africa

Contents

This is the story of incidents in the life of the author—an evangelist, convention speaker and Bible teacher.

It takes you to five continents and will simply thrill you as you read of humorous incidents and solemn moments.

Stories of his youth in South Africa, of travel, of camping, of encounters with snakes, of college studies and later ministry, of evangelistic endeavours, of convention gatherings, of meetings large and small in many places and of God's mighty operations by his Spirit again and again.

Many more stories could be told, but then the book would be too long!

Read and enjoy these, oh, so personal events, be encouraged, and respond to the numerous challenges throughout the book.

**Fred and Elizabeth
Peckham**

❝❞ Origins

The wedding bells rang out!

Farmer Robert Fairbairn led his twenty-three-year-old daughter, Elizabeth, down the aisle to meet her eager fiancé, Fred Peckham, just two years her senior, in St. Bartholomew's Church of England, Gray's Inn Rd., Middlesex. It was 25th July, 1861.

This was the beginning of an adventure greater than either of them had ever imagined.

Fred was the eldest of five children. The Leigh baptisms, Kent Archives, Maidstone, tell us that his grandfather Michael Peckham was born in 1787. His parents, Edward and Sophia, lived in Tunbridge Wells with their family of three boys and two girls, but this family was soon to be scattered to what was then perceived to be the ends of the earth. Following in his father's footsteps, Fred was a wheelwright and Elizabeth, a teacher.

The new land of South Africa beckoned as an attractive option for young adventurous empire builders, and this family of Peckhams was soon to take up the challenge and launch out into the unknown.

Just a few months after their wedding, Fred and Elizabeth, with Matilda, his sister and her new husband Harry Saunders, excitedly boarded the good ship *Cataraqui* and set sail for South Africa. It was a momentous event.

The hazardous journey took three months. Some days they were almost becalmed but on others they were severely tossed about in rough weather. In fact in one terrible storm when every thing that could move came tumbling down and rolled around, they feared for their lives. Passengers helped where they could and Fred was publicly commended and thanked by the captain for his brave efforts in the storm.

At last the Bluff was rounded and before them lay the huge bay of Port Natal. There were no docking facilities and the ship was met by numbers of little boats manned by Zulus clad in loincloths or *bheshus* (leather flaps). Horrified, Elizabeth looked over the side and exclaimed, 'I am not trusting myself to those savages!' But, together with all the others, she clambered down into the boats, helped by the friendly Africans, and was rowed to the sandy shore and then carried by the Zulus to the dry land of what was to become the great port city of Durban. It was 4th November, 1861.

Eighteen months later, two more of the young Peckhams, Tom and Emily, with their spouses, arrived in Durban, and in 1865 their parents, Edward and Sophia, with their teenage son Edwin (ten years younger than Fred), disembarked in Durban to complete the family migration. This family was to be the nucleus of a generation which was to spread its roots throughout Natal.

Fred and Elizabeth trundled inland on very uneven tracks by ox-wagon, the only means of transport, to Pietermaritzburg about sixty miles away and two thousand feet above sea level, passing as they did so the marvellous sight of the Valley of a Thousand Hills.

FARM LIFE

From 'Maritzburg they ventured a little further and settled on the farm, *Success*. It was here that Elizabeth became concerned with the welfare of the increasing number of children on the neighbouring farms and on her own account opened a small school for their benefit, and became responsible for their instruction. They were not there very long, however, before they acquired, for ten shillings an acre, the farm *Green Kopje*. It was 1147 acres in size and was situated about twenty-five miles (40 kilometres) from 'Maritzburg, near to the new village of York which had been laid out with streets and plots of land for homes and was now a well-established little town. In time, it was to boast a boarding school, a Methodist church, an Anglican church, a library, a few business premises and the homes of these intrepid early settlers. Tom and his wife settled here and it was to York that their parents came.

Green Kopje became home, the place where Fred and Elizabeth reared their eight children, four boys and four girls, and where this section of the Peckham clan took root. It soon became known for its warm-hearted hospitality and wide open door. Situated in the beautiful rolling hills of the Natal Midlands, it nestled in the foothills of Blinkwater Mountain, the end of the Karkloof range. These hardy settlers felled and cut by handsaw all their requirements from the Blinkwater forest five miles away. Even their firewood had to be cut and transported from the bush. The adjacent farm of *Summer Hill* was taken over and developed by brother Edwin. The brothers came to be numbered among the pioneers of the wattle-growing industry in Natal.

Their *Green Kopje* homestead was protected from wild animals and from wandering cattle by a stout prickly pear hedge planted all around the farm buildings. It was a tremendous achievement when Fred succeeded in supplying the household needs with an abundant flow of fresh running water. The homestead stood on the brow of a hill which sloped away steadily on either side, yet without the aid of a single survey instrument he gravitated water from a far-off spring to the house by means of a furrow over a mile and half in length. From its constant supply it was possible to establish a highly productive vegetable garden and an orchard with numerous types of fruit.

The Methodist church in York was built at first with timber from the forest, and later, when folk were more financially able, a permanent chapel was erected. Tom, who had a butchery in York, devoted much of his energies to the cause of this, his spiritual home. He was a loyal and diligent member, being the Society Steward from the day of its inception. His wife, Harriet, conducted the Sunday School choir and was fully involved in this field of service.

A leopard had been ravaging the livestock, so several men set out with their muzzle loaders to destroy it. They came upon it in a copse on the York Common just off the boundary of *Green Kopje* farm. The first volley only succeeded in wounding the animal and it turned upon Edward, severely mauling his right shoulder before the others could deal with it. Edward, the father of the clan, died a few days later from the wounds he had received. His grave was one of the first to be dug in the York cemetery. Sadly, he was not destined to enjoy the new land for long.

Elizabeth lost her first two children for lack of milk, but the third child, Robert, was kept alive partly because Fred bored a tiny hole through the tip of a cow horn, and baby Robert could suck away to his heart's content from the 'bottle'. There were no teats in those days, but this improvised one certainly worked!

The four Peckham boys were all keen sportsmen. Being excellent shooting competitors, they formed the solid core of the team of the York Rifle Association. Tennis, however, was their chief delight. Near to the house was a grassy patch which they hoed clean, leaving the strips of grass as the lines of the primitive tennis-court. That was how they began. Eventually, Bill rose to the Natal singles finals several times but unfortunately never won the title, and he and Bertie played in the Natal doubles final. This tennis court was later developed and saw many wonderful games of tennis down the years as many folk came to enjoy an afternoon or a day of tennis at *Green Kopje*.

One day, as a young man, Bertie was walking in the garden and a snake struck him in the lower leg. He ran to the house, but by the time he got there, his leg had swollen so much that they had to cut his trousers away. He drank as much milk as he could and they rubbed a caustic stick into the wound. His life was saved and he ever after kept a small caustic stick in his pocket.

Minnie, the youngest of the eight children, said, 'We had one pair of boots. If Bill went to town he wore the boots. If I went to town I wore the boots!' Those were days of intense hardship but of joy as they slowly tamed the country.

The family scattered to various parts of Natal but Bertie stayed on the farm to help his parents. Fred and Elizabeth celebrated their golden wedding anniversary at *Green Kopje* surrounded by all their children, their spouses and grandchildren, thirty-six in all. It was a triumphant occasion!

Fred died on the farm on 23rd April, 1920, and Elizabeth lived on for another seven years dying at the age of ninety in the home which they had built together nearly fifty years before. Minnie's tribute to her father was, 'He was the straightest man I ever knew!'

The fate of York is sad indeed. The new railway was to be routed through York, but the residents and those who lived in the vicinity drew up a petition against it coming through the village. The reason was that if the railway came, it would bring alcoholic drink, and the teetotal population did not want drink! So the railway was routed through nearby New Hanover. New Hanover grew and became the magisterial centre for the whole area—and York died. Today there are only two buildings to indicate that there had been any sort of activity in what had been York: the Anglican church and one house which was built by the Peckham brothers for their mother after

Edward was killed by the leopard. It is now occupied by an Indian family. In 1965 the Natal Witness newspaper ran the story with the heading, 'The Village that signed its own Death Warrant'.

**Green Kopje home and
farm of the Peckhams**

Beginnings

Bertie stayed on the farm and married Fanny Franklin in 1902, and she gave birth to a son named Ivan. She died at the birth of her second child in 1907. Bertie later married her sister, Elsie. Horror of horrors, she contracted dreaded leprosy and was removed to the leprosarium near Pretoria in 1918. She gave birth to a son in the leprosarium. Baby Douglas Fairbairn was immediately removed from the hospital lest he, too, contract the disease. Bertie visited her twice a year riding the 400 miles (650 kilometres) on horseback, spending a week with her and then riding back again. On occasions he took the train to and from Pretoria. Sad, sad days! She eventually died in 1926 and Bertie married a much younger woman, the same age as my parents, called Annie MacWilliam. We called her Auntie Mackie.

Ivan, my father, rode daily on horseback to York school, about four miles from the house, and also attended New Hanover school. Later he went to 'Maritzburg College, one of the finest high schools in the country. He then entered the bank and worked in various centres in the ten years he spent in the bank. This engagement with the commercial world gave Dad a refinement which he retained throughout life. He married Doris Gladwin from Pietermaritzburg. Her father, Ossie, came from Bath, England, as a boy, together with the three other children in the family. He was a skilled cabinet maker and played soccer for Natal. He married Sue Hall and they had two children, Doris and Oswald. Doris was also a bank employee, and after her marriage to Ivan, they returned to the farm having built a small lean-to against the main homestead building which Fred had built. I was born on 20th June, 1936. It was in this little lean-to that I spent my early years, and *Green Kopje* was my home.

Chapter 2

Oh, *Green Kopje*, how I loved you! The wide open spaces, the huge grassy paddocks with the swish of the grass against my bare legs, the wattle plantations so quiet, so soft underfoot. When the wattles flowered, their myriad tiny furry yellow flowers spread the most wonderful fragrance over the hills and valleys—right into our house. The straight mile-long gum-tree avenue to the house, the firs, the orchard, the luscious vegetable gardens, the lawns, the tennis-court, the flowers, the sugarcane, the oxen, the cows and calves, the dogs, the cats, the swimming pool in the river, the guinea fowls, the buck, and indeed the Africans who lived and worked on the farm. Oh, *Green Kopje*, you captured my heart!

What nostalgia you evoke! The felling and stripping of the wattle trees as each Zulu fulfilled his daily task, weighing the load of bark which each would produce; the crack of the high swirling whip as the Africans urged the oxen forward pulling the old wagon normally piled high with wattle bark. At times the rows of discarded boughs would be burned and the wattle trees would spring up like a forest to be hoed out leaving rows of young trees, and another plantation established. The saligna gum trees, so straight and tall, would be sold, and a hired lorry would load them from the plantations.

The thirty to forty mainly Jersey cows produced milk with a high percentage of cream which we separated and sold, giving the milk to the Africans on the farm. They sent their children who would come each morning and evening with their buckets or tins and take as much as they required. Sometimes we would play football with these children in the yard and learn the Zulu language as we did so.

We had no electricity, but the blackness of the African night was negotiated by Aladdin lamps and candles. It was fairly spooky for young children to go even from one room to another without holding the candlestick. These lights always attracted insects! What an array of moths sought comfort in the light, but their search always ended in tragedy as they drew too close to the flame.

What a rhapsody of sounds filled the evening and night air, sounds of frogs of all sizes, the 'scratch' of the crickets, the hum of insects of all kinds, and at times the deafening screech of the cicadas, the chattering of birds as they settled down for the night in the trees, at times the whistle of the reedbuck, or the bark of the bush-buck. Of course the annoying mosquitoes appeared regularly and we arose the next day with itchy bumps on exposed areas of skin. We always shook out our shoes in the morning lest some spider or other insect had made it its home for the night. The stars were so bright, and we were awed by the wonderful spectacle of the night sky, always recognizing the Southern Cross.

Thunder-storms would burst upon us in the summer months with hardly a split second between their blinding flashes of jagged fork or limitless sheet lightning followed by the crash of deafening thunder bolts—that could be scary!

We loved to watch the dragonflies and butterflies, the chameleons changing colour, the millipedes moving like stream-lined trains, watch ants scurry away, sometimes with their eggs, push a tiny insect into the funnel trap of a subterranean ant-lion and look for the lethal strike of its claw. We would flee from the fiercely biting ants called 'chegechers'. We'd watch the preying mantis make a calculated grab for its quarry, be amazed at the tens of thousands of flying ants that emerged at times after a storm, enjoy the glow-worms and the fireflies on the darkest nights, fascinated by their brightly blinking incandescent lanterns.

We would make animals of mud. They would dry and would be splendid playthings. We used the vertebrae of small animals as cars and lorries, and tied them together as trains. We built small dams in the little stream that went past the house. Dad made us stilts and we became adept at walking high. He and others helped us make kites which we flew—sometimes successfully.

Mum could cook! Her cookie jars were always full of all sorts of delicacies. And when she made mealie bread (from corn on the cob), we gathered round in the kitchen. It hardly got to the table, for the steaming bread was sliced and topped with more than adequate lashings of golden syrup—delicious.

In the evenings we would sit around the table after supper, or clamour on Daddy's knees as he read wonderful stories to us. There were always stories from the Bible written in a special children's version. And at times Dad would stalk happily around the table in the evening quoting some poetry or Shakespearean play in a manner which would make us laugh out loud.

Chapter 2

We had church once a month when the minister from far-away Greytown would come and take the service in the York Methodist church, and then the community would come out in their Sunday best. On these occasions the minister would often come to *Green Kopje* for Sunday dinner before making his way home. They were unspectacular occasions but nevertheless instilled in my young heart an awe and respect for the things of God.

On the Sundays when there was no service, as a family we would go for long walks on the farm and find a place where the hill had been dug away to make the road. Dad would help us make little roads, bridges and tunnels in the side of the bank where we played with our little model cars. They were such pleasant and loving times together.

My sister Mollie and I were growing up and the small home proved inadequate. The old galvanized metal bath was being brought into the kitchen periodically and hot water from the six-gallon copper drum on the black wood-burning stove was poured in for our bath. Our lean-to house was demolished and, right next to the old homestead, a new home was built, where we each had our own bedroom and where we had a proper bath in a proper bathroom!

Mum certainly excelled in developing the flower garden with a large range of gerberas, some of which she bred. The rose garden was always a wonderful sight, the agapanthus and the wide variety of dahlias, the red-hot pokers and the different annuals made a wonderful show.

It must have been a dreadfully anxious time when I, as a five-year-old, contracted diphtheria. I was bundled off to the Isolation Hospital near 'Maritzburg. Another boy with the same complaint and of the same age was in the room with me. His name was Heintzie. He was German and could speak no English. I was English and could speak no German, so we had all our animated conversations in Zulu! Our parents came to visit us and became acquainted, little knowing that later we would all be together in a warm fellowship as we responded to the gospel.

**Ivan and Doris, Colin's
parents**

❛❜ Growing up

W hat a wonderful childhood we had! We had loving parents and the freedom of the farm was life indeed to young boys and girls.

Our neighbours and relatives, the Wolhuters, had three children, two of whom were just a little older that we were. So our dads took turns taking and fetching us from school each day. Those six-mile car journeys will never be forgotten as we sang lustily all the way to school and back. The cars rocked to the tunes of 'She'll be coming round the mountain', 'The grand old duke of York' and a host of other popular ditties.

Sometimes we would go on picnics with the Wolhuters and others, up to the lower slopes of the Blinkwater mountain. The more adventurous would climb to the top to find the shallow lake there.

Some July holidays we spent on the South Coast of Natal and we were enthralled with the dazzle of the tumbling surf. We would race across the scorching sands to the water's edge, but hesitate and draw back from the monstrous waves and treacherous back-wash. We would swim in the safer parts and enjoy surfing with the waves. What wonders there were in the pools as we investigated the sea-anemones, the crabs, the little fish and the corals.

Mum was mistress of the piano keys and she wanted us as children to learn. We took lessons but I eventually grew tired and Dad said, 'You're just wasting my money.' I gave up. But Mum persisted and I began again, keeping going for a few years, but again forsaking the torturous path of daily practising. Again Dad terminated the lessons. When I went to high school Mum pleaded with me to begin again, and at high school I put my back into it and for years applied myself to learning to play. I will forever be grateful to my mother for persisting and pushing me to learn to play the piano for it has been invaluable in the work of the Lord.

Dad gave me a special area of the garden for myself. There I spread cattle manure and dug it all in, planting radishes, carrots, rows of peas and beans, potatoes, cabbages and cauliflowers in the fertile ground. These had to be constantly watered by hand with water carried from the garden pond, but the results were so rewarding. When only eleven years old, I sometimes rode the six miles to New Hanover on my bike with a basket of bunches of radishes and carrots to sell. It put a little money in my pocket.

Then came the honey harvest, for we had a number of hives in the orchard. Grandpa would don his bee-gear, and, with smoke to stupefy the bees, the honey would be carefully removed. In the kitchen the best combs would be set aside and the rest would be chopped into the tiniest bits, poured into a double muslin cloth and hung in front of the wood-burning stove for the night. The honey would drain through the cloth, leaving the wax in the cloth, and filling a small bath and large basins overnight. This would then be poured into bottles and sold or simply given away. We always had honey and cream on the table, and most of our vegetables came from the garden. We gathered the eggs from hundreds of our hens daily and sent them away by special egg boxes for sale.

I loved reading and would lie for hours on my stomach reading the Hardy boys, the Biggles books, the Twin books, the William books, Arthur Ransome's romances, and a host more. One bedroom wall was adorned with shelves of my books. I still have all my school reports. They make interesting reading. One word crops up in so many of them, 'conscientious', so I must have impressed the teachers that I did do a bit of work sometimes! At high school I was tennis captain of my house, and played all the sports of the day. My best academic year was the penultimate high school year when I came seventh out of the 150 boys in the year. The final year was merely a swot to the end!

SNAKES

Snakes! What African story would be complete without snakes? Walking in the plantation one day Grandpa stood for a moment and felt something whip around his leg. With tremendous presence of mind, he said to himself, 'I'm standing on its head or its tail,' and slowly he pulled up his trouser leg to see. Fortunately he was standing on its head which he ground into the earth, and the snake was no more.

Grandpa used to catch snakes and send them to Fitzsimmons in Durban for the making of anti-snakebite serum. He would pick them up and into a box they would go—a box clearly marked 'Live Snake'. How the railwaymen handled the box is open to conjecture!

As a little toddler, I gurgled and stooped down to play with an audacious snake that had slithered into the house, but I was scooped away from danger by auntie Mackie who promptly killed the intruder. The cry 'Nyoka!' (Zulu for snake), immediately got everyone's attention! Dad and I were walking in the wattle plantation one day and there by the side of the path were two beautiful yellow and black puff-adders, both curled up. He immediately terminated their existence! I was riding my bike slowly between some peach trees in the orchard one day and when I looked down, there at my bare foot at the bottom of the pedal stroke was the head of a snake. I leapt away as fast as I could, found a stick and killed it. When I held it up another smaller snake slid out of its mouth! It had obviously swallowed its mate. On many occasions we encountered snakes and dispatched them for the benefit of all. Dad once shot a black mamba, one of the most poisonous snakes on earth, high up in the wattle trees. The mamba slithered to the ground, all six foot of it, and we saw that the bullet had gone right through its head—some accuracy, as its head is only the size of a man's thumb.

Peter Wolhuter, our cousin from the neighbouring farm, and I were playing and walking one day. There was a high bank where the road cut into a small hill, and on that cutting was a tiny ledge which we, as eleven-year-olds, negotiated. We thrust our sticks into the side of the earth wall and watched the clods go tumbling down. Suddenly as we did so, a snake fell out of a hole in the wall and made straight for me. I leapt down to another small ledge six feet below, and then down to the ground. Peter hooked the snake with his stick and sent it soaring over my head onto the road. Then followed a most marvellous and spellbinding sight. The little fox terrier went for the snake. Both knew that it was a life-and-death struggle. We stood fascinated as the dog dived in and the snake struck. The dog would leap back and in again as the snake struck again and again, missing by inches. It was awesome! At last the dog grabbed the snake and his head whirled with incredible speed. It bit through the snake and the snake snapped in two. One half went flying to the other side of the road. The titanic battle was over!

One day Mollie, my sister, and I were playing in front of the house while the family was sitting on the verandah, watching us as they talked. Suddenly a night adder slithered from a low dry-stone wall and struck Mollie on the foot. In a moment Grandpa had her on the table and administered his caustic stick to the wound. The snake was killed but Mollie had to get to a doctor—fast! A massive storm was brewing. They tried to phone the doctor who lived nearby, but he was away. The rain came down in torrents. There were two doctors in New Hanover—to them she must go. The telephone lines were down on account of falling trees, so no doctor could be traced. Dad had a bad attack of gout, but he and his brother Douglas, together with Mum and Mollie, raced off to the doctor. It was a serious tropical storm and trees had fallen across the road at one point. They hacked their way through with an axe which had fortunately been left in the car. The car slithered all over the very muddy road, but they eventually arrived at the first doctor's surgery only to find that he was away for the week. On to the next doctor, but here too they drew a blank for he was also away. Back they came to the farm. What now? I was weeping—was my little sister going to die? They once again phoned the nearby doctor who answered the phone as he walked into his house. We were with him in minutes and he gave Mollie the injection which probably saved her life. She was a very sick little girl for several days. High Drama!

Birds—there were hundreds of them. You could hear them from three-quarters of a mile away as they settled in the evening in the reeds at the river. They were small finches and others of like size with brilliant colours together with the long-tailed black *sakabulas*. We sometimes hid in the reeds to witness their enchanting nightly arrival, admire their beautiful colours and listen to the cacophony of sound they produced. And then there were the little weaver birds (in Zulu called *amahlokahloka*) which would congregate in colonies and build their swinging nests high in the wattle trees. We would go to their nesting places at times, gaze with rapture at their skill, and listen with amazement to their deafening noise. Guinea-fowl there were a-plenty and we would shoot one for the pot every now and again.

BIBLE INFLUENCE

Grandpa, Uncle Ron Peckham and Dad were great tennis players and they would at times have inspiring tennis days with numbers of folk coming. At the end of these days when the visitors had gone, often with cream, honey and a boot full of vegetables (and firewood should they need it), we would sometimes gather around with Mum at the piano and sing hymns. Uncle Ron, man of God that he was, used to read the Bible and say a few words. These evenings inspired my young heart, but of salvation I yet knew nothing. We had religion and good moral values but not much more.

Auntie Mackie, who had no children of her own, had a sister named Chrissie who had several children. They all spent many holidays with us on the farm. What fun we had! Tennis, marbles, cutting and eating sugar cane from the few acres that we had for winter cattle feed, going for long walks together, swimming in the pond in the river with Dad supervising, playing police and robbers and chasing each other in the yard and in the plantations, climbing trees, playing monopoly and a host of other things. Auntie Mackie helped us organize mini-concerts which we held for the family and neighbours.

They were wonderful days! But the most wonderful of all was what auntie Mackie did each morning. She rounded us all up and sat us around the table with Bibles. For an hour each day she instructed and prayed with us so lovingly, beautifully and movingly. Her greatest quality was her love. She knew nothing about Sunday School work, but she loved! She loved God and she loved us and we knew it—and we loved her. She brought true religion into our home and made it so easy for us to follow Jesus. Now retired, I look back to those days and find that almost every one of those who sat around that table is following the Lord. We are auntie Mackie's children.

The Jersey herd of cows was there for the cream. When a bull calf was born it was simply slaughtered as it would never develop into a beef animal. Some of the cows were owned by Mum and some by auntie Mackie. I knew that auntie Mackie had given a lot of money to missionary work. Very few knew that. But one day she said to me, 'God is no man's debtor. The last sixteen of my cows that have calved have all given me heifers.' That is impossible but it happened! Her section of the herd increased considerably. God has amazing ways of rewarding his own.

**Mollie and Colin with
Peter Pentz**

**Toc H Hall where Colin
trusted Christ**

🔖 Salvation!

The break had to come. I was thirteen years old and had to go to high school. What better place than my father's school, the great and historic 'Maritzburg College? I have always been grateful that I went to College. It formed a foundation to my whole life. Off I went to boarding school, away from home for the first time. It was traumatic. I wept secretly for months, as homesick as could be. Slowly I got over it and began to enjoy the College programme—and it was great being a boarder! I slept in dormitories with those who, in a very few years, would be rugby and cricket Springbok players. The school was geared for sport.

As to religion there was the slow crocodile to the churches on Sunday morning, and the sonorous voice of the Methodist minister droned on, little of which was understood. On Sunday nights the greatly honoured but pompous head-master, John Willie Hudson, a Roman Caesar if ever there was one, led our boarding school in Anglican-type evensong. An opera singer himself, he sang with great gusto, and we got to know the Apostle's Creed and certain passages of Scripture. There was not much more for the soul at College I am afraid. The boys were as godless as ever, and swearing and blasphemy were the order of the day.

I always honoured my parents' high moral principles and tried ever so hard not to swear. In fact when I did, I would strike my arm with the knuckle of the other hand. Each word had a certain number of blows and sometimes my arm was black and blue as I tried to rid myself of swearing. I succeeded but found that the better my life became outwardly, the less peace I had inwardly. My reformation was not doing me any good. I was disturbed and longed for some means of acquiring peace. One Sunday I attended a special meeting in a church with my parents and at last I heard the clear gospel. I knew that I had heard what I wanted. How was I to get

Chapter 4

it? I had not grown up with Sunday School, or choruses, or evangelical talk of any kind. But now I had heard something which stirred my heart, and I wanted it!

THE AFRICA EVANGELISTIC BAND

In my second year, 1951, I returned home for the half-term break in May, to find that two young men of the Africa Evangelistic Band, an interdenominational evangelistic society, were staying with Grandpa and Auntie Mackie and holding an evangelistic campaign in the Toc H hall in New Hanover. What on earth was an evangelistic campaign? It was Auntie Mackie who opened the door for them to come, and now it was church every night! This was enough for a whole year! My young sister, who was still in primary school and stayed at home, sat in the back of our old Dodge car with me as we trundled along to the meeting that first Friday night. She had found the Lord in these meetings a few days before. She said to me, 'When are you going to give your heart to the Lord Jesus?'

I answered, 'I don't know—it's hard.' I did not know what she was talking about. 'Give your heart to Jesus?' I had never heard such language. Although I knew that I should pray and read the Bible, both of which I did occasionally but without much profit, to hear this, was something quite out of the ordinary.

I sat in the meeting and listened and was enthralled. Yes! This was it! I needed to come to Jesus—but how? I was to be at home for only three nights and so I thought that if the men did not speak about salvation on Saturday night I would ask them to do so on Sunday night, for I did not know that I could simply come to Jesus and that he would receive me. Fortunately Peter Pentz preached on John 1:12 that night and explained how we might receive the Lord Jesus and become his children. After the meeting I went to him and we sat on a bench at the front of the hall. He read the verse again: 'But as many as received him, to them gave he power to become the sons of God.' (John 1:12).

'Put your name in there,' said Peter, 'But to Colin who received him, to Colin gave he power to become a son of God.'

'Will you receive him?'

'Yes,' I said.

'Then open your heart right now and say, "Lord Jesus forgive my sins, come in to my heart and life, and make me your child".'

I did as he suggested and prayed that simple prayer. He looked at my earnest young face and asked, 'Has he come in? For you see, he is true to his word and will do what he says. If you are sincere and ask him to come in, he will do so.'

I nodded.

He said, 'Don't you want to thank him?'

I nodded again and simply said, 'Lord Jesus, thank you for coming into my heart and making me your child.'

Then followed words of instruction and help. I certainly needed them for I was headed for a school of boys who had no time for God or his Word. As I walked to the door a young girl named Jeanne, who had come to Christ that week, met me and said, 'Wonderful, Colin, you will never regret it.' And I never have! Wonderful day! I had passed from darkness to light. I had received eternal life and I rejoiced! It was 24th May, 1951, the same day John Wesley found assurance in 1738. I could jokingly say that my apostolic succession is intact!

That mission and another at nearby Dalton brought together those whose hearts God had touched and whose souls he had saved in an interdenominational fellowship which lasted for years and was a source of great blessing to many. It was often held in the Toc H Hall where we so often battled with the electricity generator, hoping desperately that the lights would not fail!

One night on the farm we had our evening meal with Grandpa and Auntie Mackie. After the meal Grandpa went to his room and returned with the Bible. Without a word he opened it and read. Then he prayed. I still remember some of the phrases he used in that memorable prayer. Afterwards Dad and I walked together in the dark the few yards to our home and I said, 'Dad, I have never heard Grandpa pray before.'

'Son,' he replied, 'I have never heard Grandpa pray before either.' But Grandpa had met God! The blessing spilled over onto the farm for Grandpa invited preachers, often Christian farmers with a good knowledge of Zulu, to come and preach to the Africans on the farm—there must have been about eighty Africans in all—so they came. Meetings were held, all in Zulu of course, in the huts of the Africans, and several were truly converted. They had a large part of the farm where they grew their maize and other vegetables and where they herded their cattle. We would go across to their area in the darkness, carrying a lamp, and speaking to them in one of the large huts. Sometimes Auntie Mackie would take the meeting in Zulu.

The wattle trees were felled with axes and one day one of the men, Zondi, had a very serious accident. The axe slipped and cut his foot—badly. Blood was flowing freely. In the dark they came for help. Auntie Mackie and I walked the three-quarters of a mile to the hut with torches, and there, in a weakened state, sat Zondi. She said, 'If this blood does not stop flowing, you will die.' He knew that. They had applied pressure and had done what they could, but it continued to flow freely. 'Only God can save you now,' she said, and bowed her head and prayed. 'Lord, save this man's life and stop the blood flowing.' It stopped! She used what medicines she had, binding the foot with bandages, and we walked home, rejoicing in the wonderful working of God. It was the talk of the neighbourhood for months. Auntie Mackie was in touch with God!

OTHER SPIRITUAL INFLUENCES

Back at boarding school I continued to learn and to play sport as I always had done. Cricket, rugby, swimming and tennis were all participated in with a will. Amazingly, there was no Christian meeting in the school, so I approached the headmaster. 'By all means, my boy, start your Christian meeting,' he boomed. I took my life in my hands and pinned a notice to the main school notice board. 'There will be a Christian meeting in the science laboratory on Wednesday at 12.30pm.' Who was to speak? I would take it on—only four or five months old! Not expecting more than a handful of boys, I entered the tiered hall to find it bursting at the seams. They filled the place! Oh my! Oh my! How would I handle it? I was amazed to find that the Lord gave me great liberty and I spoke from my heart giving them my testimony. I was saved and I knew it! And then they got as much as I understood of the gospel. There were no holds barred in that proclamation. It was heaven or hell. How I said it and what I said, I do not know, but at the end I made an appeal for any who wanted to come to Christ to meet me on the terraces after school. Three boys came. I don't think that they got anywhere with God, but the fire was already burning in my heart. Boys, girls, men and women everywhere must be saved! Later others came and helped with the meetings and that Christian meeting is still going strong!

Young as I was, God was speaking to me about 'full-time' Christian service. One special Sunday morning three months after my conversion, I asked the Lord to please confirm his intentions. When the minister emerged to take the service, another preacher, Peter Connolly from Wales, was in the pulpit with him. I had a sense that God was saying to me, 'Just as this man has come into the pulpit to preach, you too will be a preacher.' That afternoon I walked back to the College boarding house. As I walked down the hill, passing the high wall of a girls' high school on my right, I had a strong sense of God's leading that one day I would preach the gospel. I did not dare say this to anybody for I had never heard of anyone going to the mission field or to the ministry. I had never been in a missionary meeting. I was ignorant of the evangelical world and its activities. Who was I to think that God would call me? I shrank from that which I was vaguely, yet definitely, perceiving. Yet somehow I knew, and I was thrilled at the prospect.

Dear Uncle Ron Peckham, realizing that I needed nurturing and spiritual feeding, suggested that I attend the Baptist church on Sunday mornings where the evangelical message rang out clearly, so I went to the early morning Bible Study for my age group and then to the Baptist morning service. In the afternoons I went to his home. Those Sunday afternoons were precious. He had a great love for the Bible and he imparted that to me as he taught me for at least an hour and a half every Sunday. How I loved him for investing so much time into my young life. We prayed together and studied together and loved each other in the Lord. This was one of the most formative periods of my life. His influence remains.

Another huge influence upon me was the life and ministry of Rev. Bernard Johanson of the African Union Bible Institute, at Sweetwaters, near Pietermaritzburg. He held camps at the Bible School for young people between Christmas and the New Year each year. Mollie and I attended about eight of these camps. They were Bible camps and we certainly received choice and wonderful teaching from Mr Johanson and from other missionaries. Three teaching meetings each day with no short sermons—and we drank it all in! Every year there would be moments when God came down upon that camp, when our hearts were broken and when the tears flowed as we met God afresh. It was a source of tremendous blessing and strength to all who attended.

**Cedara College of
Agriculture**

🔊 Cedara

S uccess at 'Maritzburg College spurred me on to study further. I would take the two-year diploma course at the Cedara Agricultural College and then go back to the farm to help my dad. The call of God was somewhere in the background, but not directing me at this moment.

THE LORD'S DAY

We drove up to the imposing buildings and there I read my room allocation. There were to be three of us in one room, one of whom I knew to be a wild character. I said out loud, 'You're in for a hard time, Peckham, my boy.' That night we unpacked our cases. I knew that I would have to take a stand from the very beginning, but how, and when? The swearing and blasphemy streamed forth from these two likeable fellows. What should I do or say? At last both of them went out to the bathroom, and I fell to my knees at my bedside. I don't think that I said anything to the Lord that night. I just waited anxiously—or was it fearfully?—for them to return and see me on my knees. Their steps came down the passage and stopped abruptly at the door. I felt their eyes boring into my back. I am sure that they had never seen anyone on his knees before. 'What strange creature is with us in this room?' I could almost hear them wondering. I rose and the conversation was strangely muted, but it all picked up and we became the best of friends. I had nailed my colours to the mast from the very beginning.

Then followed lectures and studies, practical groups for field work, tennis, water polo, cricket and rugby. I went to the cricket nets for practice and saw the next day that my name was listed in the first team to play on Sunday. I was in the recreation room playing a game of table tennis when the cricket captain walked in. During a break I went to him and said, 'I am sorry, but I won't be playing on Sunday.'

'Why not?' he exclaimed.

'I am a Christian and I serve the Lord on Sundays. I will be in church,' I said.

I can still see the curl of his lip as he scornfully glared at me. 'You're not one of those are you?' he spat out, and walked away in disgust. That was the end of my cricketing career. But it was all a tremendous experience. We crammed for exams till the early hours, as all students do. We went on tours and enjoyed all sorts of experiences. Our practical group of ten had two main topics of conversation: girls, and when it turned dirty, I would protest, so then we would talk about religion! So I had great opportunities to witness to my friends. The pressures, however, were great. It was all I could do to keep my head above water and to keep clean. The battle was fierce. My lifeline was to hitch down to 'Maritzburg, twelve miles (twenty kilometres) away, and meet with the children of God. The fellowship there was sweet and so strengthening! Dad bought me a car and that made things easier.

The group of young people meeting at the Baptist church was an inspiration. They loved the Lord and gathered after every Sunday evening service and any other service in the home of the McGees who had three young lads in the group. The house was only a few hundred yards from the church so we piled in there and gathered around the piano with young Alma playing brilliantly, and later, after she had left for the mission-field, my sister Mollie took her place at the piano, with us all singing our way through Alexander's song-book. Oh how we sang! The words thrilled us; being together thrilled us; and loving the Lord thrilled us. And from that warm-hearted group, several scattered to the ends of the earth in the service of the King.

All the time I was memorizing the Navigators Scripture Memory System—110 verses which I learned off by heart with their references. I knew them backwards and investigated the contexts of so many of those texts. I got to know the biblical text. I have done a great deal of study in my life, but I must say that that memory course was the most blessed course of study I have ever undertaken. I suppose that it came just when I needed to be exposed to the Word and when I was open to receive the teaching those verses gave. It was a great preparation for later biblical study. I vowed there and then that if I should ever be in a position where I could teach, I would make my own 'Soulwinner's Bible Memory System'. I named it then and was able to work it all out and introduce just such a course to both Bible colleges at which I later lectured. It transforms preaching, for the verses are ready in your mind and mouth!

I was frustrated with my spiritual progress. There were times when I felt that I was on top of the world but there were others when I experienced such defeat. I could rejoice with the folk in Pietermaritzburg, but then I would be saddened by inner problems. I gave myself to more reading of the Scriptures and to prayer. I would go for walks and seek God with all my heart to live a life which would honour him in every part. I would spend hours in prayer all alone, but there was no relief. I was in dead earnest but could find no way through.

Then a preacher from Wales, Rev. Maynard James, appeared on the scene. His meetings were dynamic. I responded to the appeal at the close of one of the meetings and he dealt with me and others in the vestry. I expected more, but he simply directed us to the Scriptures and urged us to believe what God said and to trust him for deliverance and cleansing. I did so and left wondering, and hopefully trusting. I was given a lift to the end of the College road and had to walk the mile to the College buildings. The first few hundred yards was a dusty road and as I walked I was aware of an enormous sense of God's presence—so much so that I sank to my knees into the thick dust at the roadside. I must have been there for at least forty minutes as wave after wave of God's love and Spirit swept over me. It was a mighty experience.

Amazingly I found great relief and wonderful freedom in the Lord. I experienced victory that I had only dreamed about. For three months I continued in victory and then was tripped up by the very study of the Scriptures themselves. I thought that I had committed the unpardonable sin. My joy disappeared and my liberty in the Lord was gone. So I know that whatever heights one attains in the spiritual life, it is possible to lose it all. To get back to what I knew to be possible was an awesome struggle. In fact it took two years of wandering in the thick darkness. On one occasion at home, I wrote a letter to my parents saying that I was sorry but I would simply have to end it all. I left the letter on my desk, took the .22 rifle and went down to the plantation. The thing that stopped me from pulling the trigger was something that I had read from the pen of R.A. Torrey which stated that if you think that you have committed the unpardonable sin, that is the surest sign that you haven't done so. I did not understand it, but it stood me in good stead!

I tried to get back to victory many times. Long hours I would spend alone seeking God. After a meeting in Pietermaritzburg one night, I sat in a car and opened the Word to 1 John 1:9. 'If we confess our sins, he is faithful and just to forgive us our sins, and to cleanse us from all unrighteousness.' I said, 'Lord, my sins are forgiven. I don't know what cleansing from all unrighteousness means, but I am trusting you to do that in me now.' I got out of the car expecting the same emotional experience as had occurred on the dusty Cedara road, but nothing happened. And in the following days—nothing happened! All I knew was that I had trusted the Lord and was holding on grimly to that verse of Scripture.

One week went past and another. Three weeks went past and I was still holding on to the verse. It was now becoming a pillar in my heart. One day something happened at which I would normally be angry—but I wasn't. This sort of thing happened again. And then it began to dawn on me. 'Didn't you trust God three weeks ago? Can it be? Has God honoured his Word?' I began to walk carefully and wonderingly. Yes, God had come to this poor soul and was doing his own wonderful work in my heart. Slowly as I continued to trust and obey, the days grew brighter and the load lifted. There was no blinding flash, no mighty awareness of God's presence. It was simply a walk of faith. It was the Word in which I was trusting that brought release, and God led me out by degrees to clear heavens and to the joy of the Holy Spirit as I continued to trust him. That was the beginning of a walk in holiness empowered by the Spirit of the Lord. Praise him!

There were no Christian meetings in the college, so the very few of us who knew the Lord gathered on occasions for fellowship. In the second year I was in a room with one of those with whom I spent the first year—the wild one. His name was A.G. Payn and we all called him Aggie. We were now great friends. As I went out to one of our fellowship gatherings I handed him a tract saying, 'Read that—it will do you good.' He had observed how I lived, how I read the Bible daily and prayed, and this had had an impact far more than I could have thought. An hour and a half later I returned and found him still studying the tract, now a very concerned young man. We talked until the small hours of the morning. He was such a fine young man, captain of the cricket team and in the first rugby team, a leader in all respects with plenty of character and drive. His uncle had been a Springbok rugby player and his father should have been. His whole wealthy family was given over to sport and this was his big sticking point. 'If I become a Christian, I will disappoint my father, for it will curtail my sporting activities. I will have to see my girlfriend first.' We met together with his girlfriend in the Botanical Gardens and talked all Sunday afternoon. He was so close—so close, but he never came. Truly, he was like the rich young ruler. We parted eventually the best of friends but he was killed in a motor accident some time later. I wonder if he ever responded to the gospel.

GOD'S CALL

At Cedara the call was submerged somewhat, but one evening God spoke to me in my bedroom from Isaiah 42:6, 7: 'I the LORD have called thee in righteousness … to open the blind eyes, to bring out the prisoners from the prison …' And from Isaiah 49:8, 9: 'I will … give thee for a covenant of the people … that thou mayest say to the prisoners, Go forth; to them that are in darkness, Shew yourselves.' The words burned their way into my heart. I stood there with the Bible in my hand and with the glory of God in my soul. My roommate (Aggie), came in, took one look at me, and stopped dead in his tracks with his hand on the door handle. 'What's happened to you?' he said. I showed him the verses, and with awe, he said, 'Then you can't stay here. You must go.' That night God sealed the call of God to my soul—I knew! I was still fearful of testifying to the call, for who was I that I should be called of God? Other verses confirmed it all, yet I wrote an eight-page letter to Mum and Dad telling them of my fears and doubts and saying that I had so many deficiencies, was no good at all and would not be able to preach. I am so glad that God just blew upon all my excuses and sent me forth with a burning message in my heart.

As students at Cedara, we had done so much together and now it was time to part. The great focal point was the farewell dance. I had not attended any of these worldly events before but now I was pressurized: 'You must come! We're going to get you a blind date!' I resolutely refused and the great night arrived. The beautiful girls in their beautiful gowns emerged from the cars and were there in all their glory. It was electric! The music swirled away, and I was in the large building all alone. Alone! Alone! What was I to do? It was painful not to be with all those with whom I had had so many great experiences throughout the course. Why, we should all be celebrating together. I left the building and walked up the valley in the moonlight. I sat on a rock on the edge of the track on the farm about a mile away from the college buildings. I looked over the valley, bathed in beautiful moonlight, and sang one hymn and spiritual song after another. God comforted my heart. I, like David, encouraged myself in the Lord (see 1 Samuel 30:6). My soul was refreshed and lifted up in his presence, and I returned a few hours later with the joy of the Lord ringing within me. 'Love not the world, neither the things that are in the world,' says the Bible (1 John 2:15), and I proved that the Lord could compensate in an abundant manner.

The graduation took place and we drove away. I turned to my sister as we sat in the back of Dad's car and said to her as we drove through the gates, 'God has told me that it will be two years, and then I will be in his service.' And that is what happened!

BACK ON THE FARM

For two years I worked very happily with my father on the farm. Mollie was preparing for nursing and was with us for a year as well. It was such a delight to be together as a family unit for so long. After work most days, I would have a wash or bath and then go to my room where I would study for at least and hour each day. I revelled in the commentaries, and studied books of the Bible with them. I was engrossed in the writings of R.A. Torrey, A.W. Pink, Norman Grubb, Oswald Smith, Andrew Murray and many more. I realized the worth of getting to know the Word of God and was greatly helped by these writers.

There were many interesting incidents. Let me mention one:

Auntie Mackie had to be taken into Pietermaritzburg to meet someone who was to take her north. The time arranged was 5.00am. I drove her to town and returned not knowing that in my absence there had been a sudden heavy downpour just over the farm and further on. I did not know that the farm roads were a sea of mud. I was driving along on the dry hardened surface almost to the farm when suddenly, to my horror, I found myself sliding all over the place. The wheels left the hardened tracks and sank into the mud. Try as I would, the car would not budge. I was stuck in red mud. The time was 5.45am and it was just getting light. I knew that if I got out of the car, my clothes would be ruined, so I took all my clothes off except my underpants, and, barefoot, I stepped out into the mud. I squelched around the car and eventually found a stone which was big enough to sink into the mud and yet find a hard base. This I forced under the car and at last I had some hard surface upon which I could place the car-jack. The car rose. I was able to fit the chains around the back tyres and try to fill up the cavities beneath the tyres, kneeling in the mud. I tried again but the car just sank deeper. A little way from the road I saw some tree branches. I dragged these to the car, jacked the car up again and put as many branches as I could beneath and in front of the wheels. By this time I was covered in mud but I got into the car and at last it lifted and skidded on to harder ground. With the chains clattering all the way, I drove home. The African children had come for their milk and the machine was whirling away separating the cream from the milk. Africans were standing around, and I arrived to a full audience. I got out of the car, but there was no place to hide. I was in full view! What a spectacle, covered in red mud from my head to my toes! I darted past them all as they gaped wide-eyed, and emerged a little later transformed by the cleansing power of soap and warm water!

On another occasion my car had been on the muddy roads. Its colour was blue but it was now brown with the mud. Dad and I walked up to the end of the farm about two miles away to do a job, leaving the car beneath the huge spreading cypress trees. On our return a couple of hours later, I said, 'Look Dad, someone has washed my car. It's blue again.' We drew nearer and suddenly I realized what had happened. The African children who came every morning for milk, out of the goodness of their hearts, bless them, had decided that they would do a good turn for the boss. They would clean his car. And how did they presume to execute this grand intention? Oh, I am filled with horror even as I recall the incident. They took sacking and hessian and with that they rubbed off the dry mud from the shiny surface of the car! Imagine it! The car was covered with millions of scratches! Next morning, there they were all bright-eyed, with wide smiles, waiting for my commendation and thanks. I walked across to them and said in Zulu, 'Thank you for cleaning the car, but you see, when you clean a car you have to use plenty of water or the car will be scratched. That is the only way to clean a car! So if you ever see my car dirty in the future, never, never, never, never, never do that again!' The upshot was that I had to spray the car to bring back the shine and remove those hundred million scratches!

Chapter 5

The pulpit in the 'Maritzburg Baptist church was vacant and Rev. Johanson was asked to take over. He began a midweek Bible School in the church hall, so Mollie and I went into town on Sundays, attending both morning and evening services, and again for the two lectures each Wednesday night. It was a feast! But God was weaning me away from this warm fellowship and soon I would be off to my life's work.

The Africa Evangelistic Band had a convention in Durban and Auntie Mackie and I attended. The workers invited us to come to their daily morning prayer times and we were glad to be with them. One morning I prayed earnestly that the Lord would send forth labourers into his harvest field. 'O Lord,' I cried, 'the gaps in missionary enterprise!' I was the last to pray and as we rose from our knees, one of the workers looked at me and laughed into my face as he slapped me on the shoulder. 'My dear brother,' he said, 'you will have to answer your own prayer!'

At this time two young girls, workers of the Africa Evangelistic Band, stayed with Auntie Mackie and Grandpa on the farm, and held a campaign in the same Toc H hall in New Hanover in which I had been saved. One night a number of children responded to the gospel appeal. The girls asked me to hold meetings for them, so after the mission, I held a children's meeting each week for eighteen months before I left for Bible College. They were wonderful times and it certainly was great training and preparation for me.

I stood one day gazing at the beauties of *Green Kopje*, its gardens, its fields, its trees and everything else. I loved it! 'Lord,' I said out loud, 'you can't expect me to leave this beautiful place.' Oh, but he did, and sent me forth to gather a harvest of another kind in the world's far-flung harvest-fields.

Eventually I applied to go to the Bible College of the Africa Evangelistic Band (AEB) in Cape Town and was accepted. I went to Sweetwaters to say goodbye to Mr Johanson. I said, 'I just want to thank you for all that you have done for me. Under God you have laid the foundations of my life.'

'Well,' he replied dryly, 'if I laid them they can't be very good!' Then he continued, 'Colin, be a Bible preacher! You will find that it will work, and when it works, don't take the glory. It is the Word of God. It has power in itself.' Those words have carried me through the years, and are still indelibly engraved on my heart.

I still had to tell the Africans on the farm. They had watched me grow up. There was a strong bond between us and they all expected me to return to the farm and eventually take over from Dad. If I were to leave, their future would be insecure, for the farm would, in due course, have to be sold, and the new owner may even require them to leave and find work elsewhere. Our *induna* (chief man) was an able Christian man who had real leadership qualities. I told him that I would be leaving to serve the Lord. He listened intently to all I had to say, then he said 'Ncona! (It is well). Then continuing in Zulu he said, 'There is nothing in this world that we should love. I am glad that your treasure is in heaven, for these things will pass away.' There was a soft yielding spirit, sorrow, yet joy at my going to do God's will. What a fine old man he was.

One night Mum, Dad and I went across with our torches in the dark to the *induna's* large hut, and many of our Africans gathered together. Dad explained that they had given me to the Lord when I was born and now the time had come for me to go and serve him. Mum gave her testimony, too, which I translated, as her Zulu was not very good, then I preached and testified, after which I opened the meeting to any who wished to speak. Several did. It was a moving evening as they wished me well, not wanting to see me go but realizing that if God had called, I must obey. Precious moments!

The last Sunday before I left, I had been asked to speak at the monthly service in the York Methodist church. Dad had his mother's Bible which I borrowed and from which I preached. She had often been in that church with that Bible. I held it up and told the congregation that it was my grandmother's Bible, the grandmother I had never known, as she had died when but a young woman on *Green Kopje*. I preached on John 3—the New Birth. It was a powerful meeting and many of my relatives and neighbours sat and wept. Never before in their lives had they seen a young boy whom they had known as a child suddenly appear in the pulpit urging them to get right with God! But here he was, now to leave them to take on another role, and gather another harvest.

AEB Bible College in Cape Town—
students in 1959, my final year

Bible School

Glenvar was the name of the Africa Evangelistic Band Bible College in Cape Town. It took two nights and three days to get there. The slow train seemed to stop at every siding, and Mum's marvellous sandwiches were simply delicious—all the way.

The change for me was enormous. From the free life on the farm I was now under authority. There were lectures, study periods, quiet times, united prayer times, open-air meetings, meetings of all kinds taken or attended by the students. Life was fairly regimented and there was discipline in many areas. Men and women students had very little to do with one another, but we all lived on the grounds and shared together in so many of the blessings of the course.

And blessings there certainly were. The commanding presence of Captain Dobbie, our principal, guiding us theologically, the godly Ethelbert Smit, and quaint, but oh, so blessed, Bertram Friend, all contributed to what we became. The beloved matron, Mrs Kellerman, had an enormous effect upon us all. Her godly life and her weekly table talks stripped us bare but built us up again and again. The lectures largely handled the actual text of Scripture. Books of the Bible were dealt with in detail so we got a good working knowledge of the Bible. Lectures on biblical doctrines, homiletics, cults and other ancillary subjects were dealt with as well. It was a good all-round training with lecturers from the campus as well as ministers from the churches in Cape Town.

The course was life-changing. We went in as raw recruits and were not only given solid biblical teaching, but were led into spiritual heights which we had not known before. We learnt the value of the 'quiet time'. We rose at 5.30am., showered and prepared for the day, then had a good hour or more alone with the Lord before the day really began. The official rising bell at 6.30am was to us a nuisance and an interruption to our devotions. Those times became very precious to us all and it was there that our characters were formed—in the presence of the Lord.

PRAYER AND THE PRESENCE OF THE LORD

Friday mornings were always given over to united prayer—and what times we had together! This was the heart of the course, where staff and students met with God in a wonderful way. We learnt to recognize the presence of God and we learnt to seek it. Every term we would have a half-night of prayer. On occasions these would be so blessed that, at the close of the meeting, the students gathered in groups and continued praying for another hour or two into the night. The devotional aspect of the course was quite outstanding. We were taught that without the mighty power of God we would fail in our future evangelistic or ministerial efforts. We had to be empowered by God. We had to have such an encounter with him as would cleanse us of all self-importance and self-reliance, and where we would be filled with his presence and power. It was his work to which we were called, and for that work we had to be spiritually equipped. Work done in the flesh would fail, but as we allowed the Lord to have his way with us, he would accomplish his own purposes in and through us for his glory. We needed to be cleansed and filled with God's Spirit if we were to be effective in his service. Oh, for such an emphasis in Bible colleges today!

The country was bilingual so all our conversations and public prayers took place in English one week and in Afrikaans the next. Oh dear—but we learnt quickly enough and became quite adept at the other language, learning Scriptural texts daily in the language of the week.

TAKING MEETINGS

Each week we were out dong some sort of Christian activity. Often it was in the Coloured areas of Cape Town. This was a great training ground, for these people, who spoke mostly Afrikaans, were so uninhibited that if one had difficulty in one of the two languages with which one was not so conversant, they would quickly and loudly offer the needed word, and on we would go! We cycled to some of these meetings in their homes and in halls. I cycled with my piano-accordion on my back, often against the wild south-easter, and it proved a great boon and help at the meetings.

One night we were in a hall when, while I was preaching, a young man slunk in and sat in the middle of the congregation. The noise of a mob grew ever louder and some burst into the hall with sticks. They pointed to the young man. I held my ground and told them that I was preaching the gospel and that they were to leave. They did so, but by this time the noise was deafening. The hall was surrounded. This young man was a member of a gang that had been terrorizing people and raping women as they walked home, but they were set upon by a group of home vigilantes who chased this gangster down the streets. He had darted into the hall, hoping to evade his angry pursuers. But he was seen and now they were baying for his blood! The student who was with me put his head out of the window and called out, 'You must pray for him.'

'Yes,' they replied, 'we are praying that we will get our hands on him.'

The police arrived and lifted him bodily from his seat. They marched him to the door and threw him to the mob. How he survived that short distance to the police van I will never know—certainly without a number of his teeth! So there were interesting happenings in these Coloured areas!

There were surprises along the way. The Lord would at times encourage us with his presence as we learnt to minister. We held meetings at a boys' home and one Sunday morning the Lord simply came upon us in great power. It seemed to be a shaft of eternity thrust into the scene of time. We were thrilled to have been so blessed by the Lord. He was teaching us to appreciate his presence. Each week we would take an open-air meeting at Claremont station where hundreds of mostly Coloured people stood across the road waiting for buses. Sometimes there were Africans present and then those of us who could speak Zulu or Xhosa held forth in those languages, much to their amazement.

Glenvar prepared us for Christian service both mentally and spiritually, and I thank God for the privilege of being there and of having the spiritual emphasis in all of our studies. Two years slipped by very quickly and soon we were thrust out into the harvest field.

Hallelujah! I have found Him,
He is everything to me.
How He touches deepest heartstrings
In my inmost soul set free.

O, my precious, precious Saviour,
Take my heart, it is Thine own,
O my God, I love, I love Thee!
All my life is Thine alone!

Thine to do with as Thou pleasest,
Unreserved, abandoned, free—
Yes, entirely, wholly, fully,
Ever Thine alone to be!

Blessed Jesus, precious Saviour,
Thou who reignest in my soul,
Fill, possess, control and guide me
Till eternal ages roll!

                              —C N Peckham

💬 Consecration

I found this entry in my diary, made on 24th April, 1961, in my second year in the work of the AEB. I was then twenty-four years of age. It simply shows the extent of consecration which I experienced at that time. I wrote a poem and followed it with a brief testimony written in King James English. It might be profitable for folk to take this chapter and ponder it prayerfully before the Lord. It could well challenge the reader to a similar dedication and abandonment. Here it is in full:

Hallelujah! I have found Him,
He is everything to me.
How He touches deepest heartstrings
In my inmost soul set free.

O, my precious, precious Saviour,
Take my heart, it is Thine own,
O my God, I love, I love Thee!
All my life is Thine alone!

Thine to do with as Thou pleasest,
Unreserved, abandoned, free—
Yes, entirely, wholly, fully,
Ever Thine alone to be!

Blessed Jesus, precious Saviour,
Thou who reignest in my soul,
Fill, possess, control and guide me
Till eternal ages roll!

Amen! So let it be, blessed Lord. I desire nothing else in the whole wide world but to live for Thee. Thou art precious to me, more precious than any earthly tie. I love my close family with a strong love, but this can in no way compare with that strong devotion to Thee. My Lord, my Life, my All, I could not live without Thee. Thou art all in all to me. More precious dost Thou become daily. Oh, how sweet to look up into Thy face—to behold Thy glory.

Would that Thy children could all find this unfathomable bliss and glory in Thee. Would that they would sit at Thy feet, as did Mary of old, and gaze upon Thy face. Thou dost possess my soul. Thou art reigning within my heart. I am Thine, holding nothing back—altogether Thine! Every tiniest extremity of my being is Thine. I give this testimony knowing that Satan sees what I write. He is mighty, but Thou art Almighty and art able to keep me in Thy love. O Lord, Thou dost draw from my heart a great consecration. I know not what Thou hast for me, but my trust is in Thee, my blessed Lord—and Thou dost work all things according to Thy will.

O God, I thank Thee that Thou hast changed me from within. There were days long ago when I but dimly knew Thee, and slowly followed Thee. Life had its joys in Thy presence, but it also had its dark spots, but O my God, Thou hast wrought such a work in my soul, that I stand amazed at myself. Thou hast changed me on the inside. Life grows full of meaning, for Thou art the centre. Each day, each action, seems increasingly full of the presence of God.

Sometimes Thou dost appear in glory, and my soul overflows in praise and love. Sometimes it is but a quiet realization of Thy presence, a sense of deep peace within. Sometimes it is a burning heart. Sometimes the tears simply flow in Thy presence in brokenness before Thee. Always, Lord, Thou art there.

Oh how glorious to walk with God. Can it be? Amazing love! Unfathomable grace! Oh, this uttermost salvation! Lord Jesus, I bow in Thy blessed presence. Thou art worthy to receive all praise and honour and glory! Bend me to the full purpose of Thy matchless love. Yes, Lord! Yes, Lord! I bow in Thy immediate presence. Intimately nigh! Truly this is holy ground! Hallelujah! Amen!

Central and Southern South Africa (South Africa is highlighted)

Map of Southern Africa. Some place names have changed—for instance, Zimbabwe is the former Rhodesia, and Namibia used to be known as South West Africa

Pilgrim life

Workers in the AEB are called 'Pilgrims'. They normally go out in pairs, either men or women, and hold evangelistic campaigns wherever there are openings, mostly in the rural districts. The AEB has divided South Africa into districts each of which has a home which is the headquarters of that district and where the district superintendent and his family live. Converts and those who are blessed in the services are advised to return to their own churches and let their light shine where God has placed them. So the AEB is an interdenominational para-church organization existing as an aid to the established churches. It is also a faith organization, making no appeals for money and trusting the Lord to supply every need. When I entered their ranks there must have been about seventy working in South Africa, South West Africa (now Namibia) and Rhodesia (now Zimbabwe).

THE CHALLENGES OF MINISTRY

My first assignment was the Orange Free State—yes, there was an *Orange* Free State, and there is an *Orange* River in South Africa! I like to remind my Southern Irish friends who speak of living in the Free State (of Southern Ireland), and who glory in the *green* of the Southern Ireland Free State, that there is a Free State in South Africa, but it's *orange*! Orange is the colour of Holland and of Northern Ireland, deriving, of course, from the protestant Dutch House of Orange.

The Orange Free State is thoroughly Afrikaans, and the AEB Council, in its wisdom, sent this young English-speaking lad to Afrikaans OFS! I thought that I could speak Afrikaans until I heard the abbreviations and manner of speaking of the true Afrikaner. On one occasion an elderly gentleman looked at me with disdain and said, 'Is jy 'n uitlander?' ('Are you a foreigner?') As quick as a flash, an Afrikaans friend standing by came to my rescue and quipped, 'Oh yes, he has come out of Egypt!' I gave myself to the language and after four years of attempting to eliminate every trace of English in my accent, I spoke it like a *boer* (farmer). I was determined to get as close to them as I could so that I could more effectively communicate the message of salvation without the hang-ups of their prejudice against the English whom they had fought in the Boer war over sixty years before, which some old-timers remembered vividly.

After a few brief tours with the superintendent, my co-worker arrived and we set off on our adventure of faith. The superintendent filled the tank of our pick-up truck with petrol, put £10 in our hands and said, 'I'll see you in three months.' Whew! The Lord would provide—he said! Trust God—he said! And off we went.

A Christian family in Winburg had asked for a mission and we stayed there for the duration of the ten-day campaign. There were two messages each night, the first brief word to Christians, and then the main gospel message. My co-worker, Koos, graciously allowed me to take turns. He had been in the work for some time and was an experienced and able man. My, when he was in full flow, he was awesome, with his large six-foot-four frame, his black flowing hair, his black-rimmed glasses, his athletic movements, his strong uncompromising message, Koos was a veritable tornado on the platform. I am shorter at five-foot-seven and was struggling to get my tongue around those Afrikaans words. Oh, dear! After one of Koos's great messages, I turned to a woman of spiritual insight and said helplessly, 'I feel like a little boy.'

'Yes,' she said, 'but little boys grow up!'

I soon warmed to the battle and as we went from one place to the next, I found that the Lord was helping me both in the language, in the substance which I was preaching and in communication skills. We rose early to meet God separately before breakfast then Koos and I prayed together for an hour each morning. We then visited the people in their homes for two and a half hours. After lunch we rested and prepared for the evening meeting, after which we sometimes prayed on into the night. Getting souls for Christ was the consuming passion of our lives. Amazingly God helped us and souls came to Christ in place after place. Working with Koos was a delight, for he was a man of God and was so utterly dedicated. I am ever grateful to God for allowing me the privilege of beginning my Christian service with such a man and for setting my goals on the highest, right at the very beginning of my ministry.

During the eight years that I was out on the road holding campaign after campaign in various parts of the country, I worked with several men, each of whom left their particular mark on me. There was the mighty preaching of Koos Engelbrecht, the great prayer times with Danie Drotskie, the gracious humility of Dawie Brandt, the resourcefulness and meticulous orderliness of Danie Ferreira, and so on. We worked well together wherever we were and in whatever we were asked to do.

We drove from Cape Town to the Little Karroo where we, together with others, held a convention. It had rained a few days before and the dry and arid Karroo suddenly burst into glorious colours. When we drove back, almost the entire journey was simply breathtaking. It was as if the whole countryside was the botanical gardens in full flower for hundreds of miles! What a transformation! From sand, stone and little dry Karroo bushes, everywhere was filled with colour. The myriad-coloured carpet was interspersed with bushes of bright yellow and others of deep purple. We stopped every now and again to take photos. What a fantastic journey it was and how privileged we were to have seen and enjoyed it with wonder and admiration, realizing that we had seen something quite out of the ordinary. This was no everyday event. Normally the Karroo is dry, hot and dusty with no grass at all, with only the little Karroo bushes, but this time it was a riot of colour!

After a convention in the north of the Western Cape, we were to go on our annual holiday. We were to drive 300 miles (500 kilometres) south and then catch our trains home, but Dawie and I had been asked to visit someone who was about twenty-five miles north of the convention site. If we went north to see this person we would miss our trains and would lose a day of our holiday. What should we do? I was driving the three-ton truck with all the tents and equipment from the convention site. I drove into the middle of the main road. Dawie closed the gate and climbed into the cab. We looked at each other. Should we lose a day of our holiday by going to see the man, or should we just drive south? Dawie said, 'Let's go north. This is what we're called to, isn't it?'

'Yes,' I replied and turned the truck northwards.

We found the man to be a seeking soul, were able to lead him to the Lord, and then drove south to offload the tents and prepare for our journeys home. We lost a day, but the joy that filled our hearts as we drove south was indescribable. We sang and sang and sang. Truly there was singing in heaven too over this soul who had found salvation in Christ!

ON THE TRAIN

Pilgrims are 'in journeys oft'. I was journeying overnight from Bloemfontein to Pietermaritzburg by train. In my allocated compartment were two men who were cursing and blaspheming in a worse manner than I had heard for a very long time. I settled down for the night in the midst of this flood of foul language, and before I lay down to sleep, I took out my Bible, sat there in front of them, reading and praying silently. They were silenced and climbed into their beds. I said, 'You know, I love the One whose Name you have been loosely and flippantly using. He has saved me from sin and from hell, and I am serving him with all my heart.'

One lifted himself up on his elbow and said guiltily, 'I go to church now and again.' No more was said. The next morning, that man opened the conversation with, 'What you said last night hit me hard. In fact I could not sleep. I was so worried that I got up and found an empty compartment and prayed to God.' We went to that empty compartment again and I explained to him the way back to God with the Bible open before us. We got on our knees and sought God together. A pitiful backslider had returned home!

On another train journey, I was in the dining saloon when a bright young fellow, slightly physically deformed, stood at my side. 'Hello sir,' he said. I had met him somewhere—but where and when? Then it all came flooding back. A year ago, on this very route, he, together with a number of other physically handicapped boys, was in the same coach as I was, travelling home for the holidays from their special school. I had seen an opportunity and had taken my piano-accordion into one of their compartments. Of course they all piled in, about twenty of them, on all the beds which were lowered from the walls, and we sang! Oh how we sang—songs which they knew, ditties which they loved. I then taught them some simple choruses, and we sang them. I gave them my testimony and we sang again. I spoke to them about the Lord Jesus and had a wonderful time of presenting the gospel. I asked whether any of them would like to trust the Lord and begin to follow him. Two boys responded and we went to another compartment where I had the joy of leading them to Jesus. Now a year later, here one of them stood. 'Are you still following the Lord?' I asked.

'Oh, yes, sir,' he replied enthusiastically.

'And the other boy who came to Christ with you?'

'He has left the school now but he is still very much a Christian,' he asserted warmly. It pays to be alert to the possibilities and to buy up the opportunities!

VISITING PEOPLE

Several of these small rural campaigns yielded very little or no outward fruit. It was solid slog. But we were certainly learning the principles of spiritual harvesting and were being formed and fashioned into 'new sharp threshing instruments having teeth'. Visiting was an important part of it all, and these were often some of the most fruitful times. People were then able to open their hearts personally. They could seek the Lord in the privacy of their homes, and we could counsel them more effectively on a one-to-one basis. Yet on occasions visiting could be rather rough.

One hot day in the Transvaal, as I walked from house to house, a lady sitting on the front verandah invited me to sit down and have a cup of coffee. I was grateful and began to tell her of our purpose for being there, inviting her to attend the meetings. She suddenly turned on me. 'Why don't you go and get yourself a job?' she asked belligerently. We continued to talk and the conversation turned to spiritual things. No, she was not sure of her salvation. No, she did not know very much about the New Birth. No, she did not know whether her sins were forgiven. Then I turned on her—gently! 'You asked me why I did not get myself a job,' I said. 'I did have a job. I farmed with my father on our farm, but God called me to gather another harvest than that which I was gathering on the farm—and this is the harvest, the souls of men. This is my job!'

One day in the Strand, I was cordially invited into a beautiful home, but when I began to warm to my subject, the man said, 'We don't talk about religion in this house, and if you continue, then get out!' I replied that we were holding meetings in the town and invited him to attend. He rose and grabbed me by the shoulder, marched me to the front door and literally threw me down the front steps. Had I not been agile, I would have landed on my nose! I turned to the glaring figure framed in the doorway and said, 'One day, sir, you will remember that a man came to your house to talk to you about the Lord Jesus, and you rejected him. Nevertheless you are still very welcome to come to the meetings.'

Shall I ever forget the roasting that I received from a lady at Memel? She glared at me, went utterly livid with rage, poured out her wrath, exhausted her vocabulary and vented all her venom upon me for daring to come into this town when it was served by two large churches. 'I have my church and my minister—who do you think you are to come here knocking on my door?' And on and on!

Then there was the time when we visited a town a little while after the Jehovah's Witnesses had been. The lady opened the door and glared very aggressively at me. 'It's all right,' I said, 'I am not a Jehovah's Witness.'

'Well I am!' she exclaimed as she banged the door in my face.

In Namaqualand, 400 miles north of Cape Town, I joined Danie D. whose partner had to leave him. We had a very difficult time in this whole area, so much so that we withdrew at one stage and spent three days of prayer together on the farm of a warm-hearted Christian farmer. It was he, the farmer, who prayed when we left, 'Lord, let the blood on their swords never become dry!' It was a difficult time, but there were compensations. Danie had led an old couple in poor circumstances to the Lord before I joined him, and after three months we were to pass their home on our way back to Cape Town. 'We'll call in,' said Danie. We sat in the poorly equipped front room as he instructed them. It was so simple, so helpful, so instructive, so tender, so beautiful, so spiritually uplifting. God came into that room as we prayed together with the dear old couple. The presence of the Lord followed us into the car and we travelled many miles without a word being spoken—silenced by the awe and wonder of his presence. Eventually after twenty minutes or so, I said, 'Isn't it wonderful that God can pick someone up and use him like this?' Of course, I was referring to him, and he knew it.

'Yes,' he said, as the tears streamed down his face, 'and we are so unworthy.' What holy moments those were.

In Namaqualand we worked in a small village called Hondeklipbay. We stayed alone in a small empty house and held the meetings in the largest room in the house where we set out the chairs. There was no bath in the bungalow. We enquired here and there but no-one seemed to have a bath. In my letters home, I recorded, time after time, 'I haven't had a bath yet!'

By this time we were expert in dry-cleaning in a bowl of water. At last we found a house which had a bath and its owners agreed to light and stoke a fire outside the house under the drum of water. At ten on Saturday morning the bath would be ready. Just before ten, therefore, we marched across the little village with our towels over our shoulders—we were going to take a bath! Great event! Thankfully we splashed away. Immediately afterwards I went to the Post Office and sent my mother a wonderful telegramme: 'Had bath. Love, your clean son, Colin' Primitive conditions! Great to have a sense of humour!

We were in a very religious area. When speaking to one man, he simply said: 'No! No! You needn't talk to me about my soul. I was born under the cloud!' By this he meant that he was born into the people of God as the Israelites were born as God's people in the wilderness under the cloudy pillar. From this false security he would not budge.

We spoke to a woman who put all her faith in God's electing work. No, she would not be able to say how she stood with God, for only he knew that, and at the Judgement Day it would be revealed whether she was in the elect or not. At the moment she was doing all she could by trusting in the Lord. No, she had no assurance of salvation. She certainly had religion but not reality, Christianity but not Christ. I watched and listened for an hour as Dawie, my co-worker, dug her out of this pit, until she exclaimed, 'If that is so, then I am not saved.' That afternoon she found true assurance as she trusted the Lord for personal salvation. It was probably the best piece of personal work that I have ever witnessed.

We were having a very difficult time at a particular village and one night we knelt as usual at our bedsides to have our evening devotions. After about thirty minutes I just turned round, knelt beside my co-worker, and we spontaneously began to pray together. Oh, how God came to us as we prayed on into the night. I can still hear Danie D. say, ''Tis so sweet to trust in Jesus, so sweet, so sweet, so sweet.' We wept and were refreshed in the presence of the Lord.

Those were great days! There's nothing like working a mission. Knowing that previous victories cannot guarantee present success, you have to start all over again on each occasion. Conditions are different each time. As you meet the people and assess the situation, your eyes are opened to special needs in that community. Preaching is geared to these needs and the gospel is preached without fear or favour. The pilgrims bring a straight message and for this they are held at arms' length by some but embraced and loved by many. Missions lasted ten to fourteen days, or longer sometimes, and there was always a mighty battle as the workers engaged on enemy territory and battled for souls. There was the hard slog in the blazing sun as we walked the roads and knocked on doors inviting people to the meetings. These times on the doorsteps or in the homes were often profitable occasions of personal witnessing and soul-winning. Then there was the deep burden and breaking heart. To those who have walked this pathway of passion, pain and burdened intercession, it is a way of life. Not only, however, was there the burden but also the blessing, not only the agony but also the glory, with the presence of God being sensed and known in an abundant measure.

Mr Pieter Scholtz and I were taking a series of meetings in the Strand. I was giving a short message in English and he followed with the main message in Afrikaans. We met just before the meetings in the vestry. The burden of the meeting was upon us both. We prayed briefly and then sat in weighty silence. It was time to begin and as I stood up, I said to him, 'Oh, the burden!'

'Yes, brother,' he replied, 'we're called to it!'

What times of prayer! What holy fellowship! What tears! What broken hearts! Yes, and it was worth it all when souls came to Jesus! That is the life of a pilgrim—broken bread and poured out wine. It is a giving of your life to Jesus with no thought of remuneration or compensation. You just give yourself over and over again. You get applause and opposition, you get the kisses and the kicks—and you know the difference!

Amazingly, God looked after us and gave us the heritage of those who feared his Name. The choicest of Christians stood with us and we were bound together in the love of God. It was a fellowship across denominational lines, which was wholesome and enriching, prayerful and supporting, and we found that God marvellously supplied our needs. We went at his command and he was true to his Word. He will not leave you alone and forsaken. He is there—always!

**The first mission held at the
Methodist church at Winberg**

Incidents on missions

The first mission at Winburg was held in the Methodist Church but very few people attended. Nevertheless, several souls trusted the Saviour. Missions followed in quick succession, Bethlehem, Hennenman, Bothaville and so on. Numbers were small but the presence of the Lord was wonderful in so many of these meetings. There were strong battles as we sought God for the folk to come and trust the Lord. A great deal of the work was done in the homes where the needs are personally revealed and dealt with. Much prayer was offered and if the small gatherings did not influence many, God certainly used them to form and fashion us as we battled away in prayer.

At Steynsrus we pitched a tent and this drew larger numbers—in fact we began with fifty-six. On a Sunday evening after the church service, at our rally, fifteen responded to the appeal. We dealt with them as we could and they trusted the Lord for his great salvation. Some were from the boarding school. They told us later that they formed a prayer group and sometimes, even against hostel rules, they gathered after lights-out to pray together. This was a particularly blessed mission.

On house-visiting we found a seeking soul one day, and led her and her little daughter to the Lord. They attended all the meetings and rejoiced in their newfound salvation. 'Please go and see my husband,' she pleaded. 'He wants nothing to do with God.' We went to his workplace and were able to speak to him. He was angry about what had happened to his wife and daughter and almost chased us away. The mission continued and she pleaded once more, 'Please go and see him again.' We went the second time and he was more aggressive than ever. We left with sad hearts. The mission closed with a number of folk having trusted God for salvation, and we left the town. Two weeks after the mission was over, we opened the newspaper and were horrified to find that near to the town we had just left there had been a terrible motor accident where the driver, his wife and daughter and two friends had been killed as the car stalled on the level crossing. The speeding train could not stop and had crushed them all. (I still have the newspaper cutting.) It was the family with whom we had to do. The wife and daughter were transported to glory but the husband was, in all probability, hurled into a lost eternity. He had been given the opportunity to turn to God, but resisted the Lord once too often. It's a dangerous thing to resist the voice and grace of God.

At Allanridge one night I sang 'The Great Judgement Morning' and Koos preached a mighty message on the Judgment. What a meeting it was! People left stunned and silent but some remained to seek the Lord for salvation. One town after the other was visited and meetings held, sometimes on a tour and sometimes a campaign.

ROADSIDE MINISTRY

Koos and I were travelling in the Orange Free State on a dusty minor road. We came upon a group of Africans standing at the roadside gazing helplessly at their car. The bonnet was up and they looked despairingly at us as we passed. Koos was driving, and about two miles down the track, he suddenly put on the brakes and said, 'I'm going back.' We pulled up alongside the stricken car. Koos took off his jacket and delved into the engine. After about fifteen minutes the car stuttered to life and then it roared away to the cheers and shouts of the delighted Africans. They danced with joy and laughed with glee as they thanked him over and over for what he had done. But he did not leave it there. I can see him now wagging his finger and speaking so sincerely to them. 'Do you know why I came back? It is because Jesus has put his love into my heart for all people. He loves you and I love you too because of him. I only came back because, as a Christian, I want to serve him, and in helping you I am serving him.' Then he preached to them. The gospel came clear and straight and they knew that day that there was one white man who loved the Lord and in whose life they saw that love.

We were with the Rossouws on their farm near Bothaville, when an African on the farm who had become a preacher came to tell of his ministry at a recent campaign. He was thrilled at what God had done. They were so conscious of the presence of the Lord and a number had put their trust in Jesus. On and on he went, rejoicing in the Lord, and we rejoiced with him.

Then Koos said, 'Listen, Jonas, you stay a praying preacher! Do you hear? If you do that you will keep humble and God will be able to use you in the future. Stay a praying preacher, Jonas!' It was said with such conviction and the Lord was so present, that the words burnt their way into my soul, establishing what I knew to be true and which I was applying to my own life. They have stayed with me all my life.

OTHER MISSIONS

At Welkom we had a team of workers and the venue was the parking garage of a large building in the town—filled with cars during the day but empty at night. What a place to hold meetings! The chairs were set out every night and the people welcomed. Quite a number came as we took turns preaching. One night I was to speak and had prepared something which did not settle well in my heart. As I sat at the small portable organ playing the hymn before I was to speak, I felt that I could not preach what I had prepared. I stood to my feet and preached another message altogether— and it was developing as I preached it! Yet it was in my heart and God anointed the words as I spoke. They poured forth with great liberty and, at the close, I made an appeal to which numbers of folk responded. We had a great time of prayer with them all and God was greatly glorified as the car park became a hallowed trysting place. God sometimes gives us surprises when he brushes aside all our well-thought-out sermons and works in his own way.

One unique mission was held in the veldt some distance from the town of Brandfort. Our enthusiastic, retired host and hostess wanted the people among whom they had farmed to hear the gospel, so we pitched a few tents on a farm with no buildings in sight. We stayed there in the veldt where they cooked and cared for us while a large marquee was erected for the meetings. Then we invited the farming folk, driving from farm to farm—and they came. One night there was a massive storm and the ground in and around the tent was soaked as the tent had been unwittingly pitched in a slight hollow. The old couple gazed at it all in dismay. 'We will have to close the mission immediately,' they said sorrowfully. But we remonstrated: 'No! We're not closing. Where can we find some sand?' About ten miles away we came upon dry river sand and we loaded a truck full, returning to spread it all over the muddy floor of the tent. Twice more the pick-up truck made the journey and not only was the tent floor covered but the approaches to the tent as well. All day long we worked and by evening the tent was shipshape and ready for inspection. Off came the overalls and on went the suits and the preachers were ready to receive the congregation! The elderly couple were amazed and thrilled. Again there was a never-to-be-forgotten night when God descended and souls were deeply affected by the Spirit's operation. They left like wounded birds, in total silence, but none responded openly to the gospel. The battle is tough.

Danie D. and I stayed for a few days' rest on a farm in Namaqualand. The lady of the home asked us, 'Do you drink *bies*?' I looked at Danie enquiringly.

'*Bies*?' I asked, 'What is *bies*?'

He did not answer me but said to the lady, 'No, I don't drink it but give it to Mr Peckham. He loves it.' She went out to get the drink and I said to Danie, 'What is bies?'

He smiled and said, 'You'll enjoy it.' She returned with a large glass of viscous, gooey, whitish drink. I began to drink—and, oh my, I nearly brought it all up! What was I drinking? It was colostrum, that which the cow gives to the calf immediately after it is born—but this was from a goat! It is a strong creamy milk full of protein and goodness, and it tasted awful! I could not simply give it back to the good lady, having been taught to eat and drink what was put before me, so I took my life in my hands and drank the lot in one gulp, while Danie tried his utmost to hide his laughter at my expense. He got me that time!

On another occasion, Danie Drotskie and I were working in a very difficult place in Namaqualand, when God came to us both and, remarkably, on the same afternoon, as we waited separately before the Lord, gave us the same verse. We were certain that the Lord would work in power, but circumstances dictated that we had to leave the area fairly abruptly without seeing anything of what we both felt God was about to do. We had believed and had the assurance of faith, but nothing came of it. We went our separate ways and about three years later we met again at a convention. We sat together and talked over our midday meal. He had just paid a visit to the area where we had been working at that time and he said to me, 'Do you remember this one and that one? Do you remember that family and this one?'

'Yes,' I answered.

'They're saved, brother,' he said. 'They simply came to the Lord after we left and they are following him today.' It was such a tender conversation. We wept together at the table as we remembered how God had spoken to us there and given such assurance to us. We had left with such heavy hearts, but now, years later, God's word to our hearts was vindicated and he had done what he told us he would do. Faith's assurance is a very precious thing.

A farmer in the Little Karroo (a fairly arid area of the Cape Province) had three young daughters and he asked us to hold a mission in his large home as he wanted, most of all, his children to hear the gospel clearly presented and come to trust the Lord as their Saviour. Much prayer went up for this mission. We arrived and began visiting the farms in the area. About twenty-five people attended every night. We were warned not to visit a certain man who had no time for religion and poured forth a flood of obscene language constantly. So, of course, we went to see him and found him kind and docile. What he said about us later I do not know! But half way through the mission during the singing of the first hymn in the large living room, he entered with his wife and two teenage children—a boy and a girl. During the singing of the final hymn they all disappeared. But the next night they were all there again. I spoke on the topic of assurance that night, and it was one of those wonderful nights when the presence of the Lord was almost tangible. I made an appeal and all four hands went up briefly. I counselled them at the back of the room and all four trusted the Lord as their personal Saviour. What joy filled all our hearts that night on the farm. Some months later the newly-converted wife wrote to us saying that they hold family prayers every day now 'and my husband prays so beautifully!' Wonderful—it was a household salvation! And the three girls, two in their teens, all opened their hearts and came so easily, readily and beautifully to Christ.

I was on a tour in Zululand and had but one night at a certain town. The meetings were advertised beforehand but at this particular place there was virtually no interest. Only my host and hostess, the man who played the piano, the one who opened the church, and one other were present. What was I to do? I held the meeting as if there were 1,000 people present and preached my heart out. The presence of God descended upon the meeting. We left without a word. Even the car was filled with the presence of the

Lord. We walked silently into the house and the man closed the door, put one arm across my shoulders and his other arm across his wife's shoulders and said, 'My brother!' We stood in the hallway with bowed heads, and wept. God was in our midst! When you know that God is with you, you can go through fire and water. And when you have touched this, the presence of God, you are spoiled for everything else.

St Lucia is the fisherman's paradise. Beautiful St Lucia, a natural forest reserve, untouched by human development. We were working in this area and thought that it would be a good idea to pitch a tent and hold a mission for the fishermen who were coming and going. When we arrived, we were confronted by big notices: 'Beware of Crocodiles, Hippopotami and Sharks!' so we didn't take a swim! We pitched our tent and in the morning we arrived to find that the long grass around the tent had been eaten to the ground. The hippopotamus had paid us a visit. Fortunately it did not destroy the tent! On visiting a house, we found a seeking soul and led her to the Lord, but the fishermen were more interested in fish than in us, so we soon abandoned this rather futile attempt and packed our tent away.

We were on a mission in Kamieskroon in Namaqualand, about 300 miles north of Cape Town, when Dr Verwoerd, then the prime minister of South Africa, his wife and entourage paid the area a visit to see the wonders of the Namaqua daisies. The whole town went out to the vast fields of beautiful, deep yellow daisies with the prime minister. He was asked to pose with the older members of the community and photos were taken. I stood there with my camera and called out, 'Your hat, doctor, your hat!' He obligingly removed his hat for the photo. I wrote home that night telling Mum and Dad that I had asked the prime minister to take off his hat! Whew!

I worked a week-long church mission at their request in the Transvaal. It was the hardest mission I had ever worked. I seemed to be battering my head against a brick wall every night. The mission closed with no fruit whatsoever. After the last meeting I drove round to the home of the man who had been with me on the platform each night and had led the meetings, to say goodbye, as I was to leave very early the next morning. He was already in his bedroom, but came to the door and said that he would see me in the car. He put on his gown, sat in the car with me and wept. He wept for half an hour, and I said nothing. Out it came at last. 'Do you know why you have been having such a hard time? I am living in sin. The woman comes into the meeting each night and laughs at me on the platform.' Here was I searching my heart to see if I were perhaps to blame for the hardness in the meetings when all the time it was this man living in sin! His wife in the bedroom knew nothing about it. I counselled him as best I could but had to leave him to sort out the mess with his wife and with the church. Shame on us that such things should take place in the family of God. It not only brings disgrace on those concerned, but it hinders the advance of the work of God. His sin prevented the powerful manifestation of the Spirit of God, and caused the mission to be ineffective.

A Christian teacher taught in a high school in Middelburg, Transvaal. He had been witnessing and preaching very effectively among the scholars in two high schools, and felt that the pupils needed a clear evangelistic encounter. There were three other Christian teachers as well. He called us to come over and help him. It was an amazing few days. We had sessions when they were all present, and smaller sessions where we could get closer to them. At the end of those few days, over sixty young people had committed their lives to Christ, and were formed into prayer cells which were nurtured in the days ahead. The Christian teachers were thrilled!

I was on an eighteen-day tour in the Western Transvaal. It was tiring as I travelled from one town to the next, visiting as many people as I could and then holding the pre-arranged meeting. At Wolmaranstad I stayed with someone who had recently come to Christ and held two meetings in the Presbyterian church. Among those who attended there were various denominations represented, both English and Afrikaans. I held the meetings in both languages alternating from Afrikaans to English throughout the messages. The second night was a great meeting and four people of different denominations and both languages trusted the Lord for salvation. The contact with the folk with whom I stayed was greatly blessed and the bond has continued to this day.

Danie F. and I worked in Stanger, a largely Indian town. We stayed in a caravan and cared for ourselves, but our finances were very low. We had been given a tray of pawpaws, a packet of cream crackers, and a small bottle of marmalade. For breakfast, therefore, we had cream crackers and marmalade and then pawpaws. For lunch we had pawpaw and then cream crackers and marmalade, and for dinner we reverted to cream crackers and marmalade and then pawpaws! The pawpaws ripened just as we needed them, but we thought that we had better try and get something else. After a meeting one night we went to see what Stanger had to offer in terms of cafés. We passed one and then another, judging them to be third class cafés which we would not enter. Eventually we saw one which we thought might be acceptable. We went in to see what we could buy. There was a large round of cheese. 'We'll have a quarter of a pound of cheese, please,' we said to the Indian shopkeeper. He took out a huge blade and wiped it with a yellow duster. Bits of the yellow duster clung to the sticky blade. He cut a piece of cheese and handed it to us wrapped in brown paper. We took it gingerly to the caravan. 'Let me tell you now,' said Danie, 'I am not going to eat that cheese!' We nearly split our sides laughing.

'No,' I said, 'I am hungry; I will eat it.' I cut off a slice and ate it with great apprehension. The cheese stank. I barely got that piece down my throat, then put the rest of it, in its paper, on top of the caravan. We got rid of it the next day and purchased something better.

In the Strand, I preached one Sunday morning in the Baptist Church. At the door I shook hands with the people as they left. One dear Afrikaans brother who was not too conversant with English, gripped my hand in a vice-grip and nearly shook my arm off! He was thrilled with what he had heard and said enthusiastically, 'Thank you so much for that expiring message!' I hope that he meant 'inspiring'!

At Stanford, we secured a room where the lady gave us breakfast and, for the rest, we had to fend for ourselves. This meant a meagre diet and after visiting the people one day, seeing the fig trees in the various back yards, I said, 'How I would love some figs!' We knew no-one who had a fig tree, but as we walked down the road, a lady whom we had not visited, but who had heard of us, called out to us to come into her house. We did so and she sat us down at her table and gave us—what do you think?—yes, it was a huge bowl of figs! 'Before they call I will answer' (Isaiah 65:24)! Just a little thing, but how precious of the Lord to bless us in this tasty way!

At Touws River we had a very good mission with almost a hundred people attending. I knew that there were several there who had not come to Christ. I closed the meeting one night by saying in my prayer, 'Lord, if there are those in this meeting who do not know thee, bless them with a sleepless night! Amen!' A few nights later a lady who had been in that meeting, together with six others, sought God for salvation. In the testimony meeting she told how what had been prayed had happened to her. She had not been able to sleep. But she trusted Christ to come into her life, 'and then,' she said, 'I had another sleepless night for the sheer joy of what had happened!'

THE WAY TO HELL

Near Vredendal we pitched our tent in the circular grape/sultana drying platform of a Christian grape/raisin farmer, and preached each night for ten days. Some wild young people were persistent in their attempts to wreck the campaign with loud shouting and revving and spinning their cars on the gravel at the tent. They came in every night, sat at the back, and joked their way through the meeting. We had spoken kindly to them again and again, trying our utmost to get onto their wavelength, but to no avail. The last meeting at three o'clock on Sunday afternoon arrived and I had a tremendous burden on my heart for them. I said, as I stood up to speak, 'We have been telling you throughout this campaign how to go to heaven. Since that does not interest you, I am going to tell you how to go to hell.' A lady pilgrim who was with us, sitting in the front row gasped audibly. Those youngsters listened!

I reminded them that the way to hell was a *delightful* way, where you enjoyed yourself immensely and laughed the gospel away, argued the gospel away, hurried the gospel away with busy programmes, for you had no time for these things. I reminded them that it was a *deceitful* way, that the end of all the enjoyment was a slippery downward path to death. I told them that it was a *difficult* way and that they would have to work hard to get to hell. They would have to trample on traditional values of decency and morality. They would have to ignore the beautiful Christian lives which crossed their pathways. They would have to silence their conscience, and stifle the convictions of the Holy Spirit. They would have to reject earnest conversations with Christians and messages brought to them from the Word of God. They would have to trample on the prayers of their godly parents or relatives. They would have to reject God's Word. And finally they would have to reject Christ's sacrifice on Calvary. It was a difficult road and they would have to work very hard to get there. There was a deathly silence in that tent. Some of the Christians were weeping. I made an appeal and two of those hardened characters responded. We prayed with them and led them to Jesus while their friends stood silently in deep thought. I went to them and continued to challenge them for some time but there was no further response. So the campaign ended with some fruit, but we left with heavy hearts for those who simply would not yield their lives to Christ.

In the Western Cape a couple pleaded with the district superintendent to send workers for a mission. He was loath to do so, knowing these people were extremely poor and lived in a very small house on the farm. But their insistence paid off and we were sent to them. They gave us their bed— where they slept remained a mystery! They witnessed far and wide and urged the people to come to the meetings in the local hall. God blessed the mission. 'Where are you staying?' they asked. 'With them?' Christians were amazed, and food of all kinds began to arrive at their door. We fed sumptuously and in fact our sacrificial host and hostess were able to live for six months on the food received during those two weeks! God provided for us but he provided for them as well as they gave themselves to the work of God. They were thrilled to be part of the gospel team. Didn't Paul promise that God would supply the need of those missionary-supporting Christians at Philippi? They had given much to him in his evangelistic enterprises, and he assured them that 'God shall supply all *your* need according to his riches in glory by Christ Jesus' (Philippians 4:19, italics mine). God not only cares for those who go at his command, but for those who support those who go. God cares for the whole team!

There was a division of the AEB which worked among the Coloured people. Today it is an independent evangelistic society. They have a Bible college called *Bethel* in the Cape Town area and the work is simply called 'The Bethel work'. Over the years the work has been greatly blessed. They have a convention centre in nearby Paarl and I was asked to speak at a Day Conference there. The hall was filled to capacity and I poured out my heart. At the close I made an appeal and about seventy folk crowded around the platform. They wept so loudly that had I wished to pronounce the benediction I would not have been heard. I merely waved the people away while the folk at the front had dealings with God. It was a day long to be remembered as souls sought and met with God. Many years later a Christian worker, who had been there with me, reminded me of that great experience at Paarl. It is not easy to forget such a manifestation of God's power!

**The Peckham family: Christine, Mary,
Colin Neil, Heather, Colin Morris**

Snippets from missions, camps and conventions

All the workers of the AEB send weekly reports to the headquarters. Selected parts of the reports in these letters are typed into a letter which is sent to every worker every week. It is called the *Pilgrim Letter* and is an in-house publication which keeps all the workers in touch with one another and facilitates effective intercession. I searched the archives and found the reports which I had sent in over the years. I ran photostat copies of them and have included notes from them in the following selections which give an indication of the scope, hardships and blessings in the life of one worker in the Band.

I have also included a few reports from Mary Morrison, a pilgrim from the Scottish Faith Mission, who worked in South Africa at the invitation of the AEB, and who was later to become my wife. Mary comes from the Isle of Lewis, Scotland, which forms part of the Hebrides. She was saved in 1950 in a remarkable revival on the island in which Rev. Duncan Campbell was used of God. Her testimony is recorded in a book *I was saved in revival*, and in a shortened form in our book on that revival called *Sounds from Heaven*. She entered the Faith Mission Bible College in Edinburgh and completed the diploma course before going out into the work of the Faith Mission and holding campaigns in the rural districts of Great Britain. It is the mother mission of the AEB in South Africa and operates along the same lines, sending young people into the rural areas to conduct missions as an aid to the churches.

On two occasions, on the Scottish islands of North Uist and Tiree, she and her co-worker saw the hand of God move mightily in genuine revival. (The North Uist revival is recorded by the late Rev. John Ferguson, a convert of that movement, in a book called *When God came Down*.) This brought her to the attention of Christians in many places and she was released from the normal Faith Mission work to respond to calls for her ministry all over Britain and Northern Ireland. For five years before our marriage, she roamed the country responding to invitations from churches and conventions. The Young Women's Christian Association in South Africa first brought her to that country, to speak at their tri-annual meetings in the large cities of South Africa and Rhodesia (now Zimbabwe). She spoke in various places in Canada including the great Spring Convention of 3,500 people at the Prairie Bible Institute. The seven messages which she gave there were published in their monthly magazine. Later the AEB brought her to South Africa for six months to speak at conventions and campaigns all over the country. Her ministry was greatly appreciated and she was much sought after. When she first went out into the work of the Faith Mission, she read one of C H Spurgeon's sermons almost every day for five years. That reveals huge discipline and is in itself a magnificent theological training! In all she served fourteen years in the Faith Mission before we were married.

But now, back to my work in the rural areas of Southern Africa.

7.3.60 Winburg

The Prayer Convention here has just ended. We have been encouraged and inspired.

11.4.60 Winburg

Some souls have sought the Lord. Our landlady came back to God with real determination.

13.6.60 Hennenman

God has met and blessed souls at this place although at times it was a hard fight.

16.5.60 Bethlehem

It is a hard battle. Indifference and coldness is prevalent, but we have been conscious of the Lord's presence with us.

During 1961 I had to withdraw from the active preaching work for some time as my vocal chords needed a rest. Apparently I had been using my voice incorrectly. Fortunately they were not damaged beyond repair and I was able to get help from a voice therapist in Durban, later returning to the work full-time.

7.5.62 Pietermaritzburg

Mr Peckham has gone to represent the Band with his own slides of the AEB and films of AEB work in the Baptist Church Missionary Convention. He says: 'I gave a missionary address at the close of which fourteen young people responded to the appeal for Christian service.'

15.10.62 East London Missionary Convention
A great convention! There were 400 to 500 each night. I spoke on Friday night when scores of young people responded for full-time service.

19.11.62 Sasolburg
The tent is pitched in the centre of the town, notices are placarded all over, several hundred handbills have been distributed, but the response is very poor.

8.4.63 Robertson
It was a blessed mission. We dealt with several souls for salvation during the mission.

10.6.63 Letter to headquarters
It has been such a blessing to be out in the fight again. There's nothing like it in the whole wide world—fighting for souls in the Name and in the power of our Conquering Jesus!

9.9.63 Springbok
The Springbok Convention, though small, was marvellously blessed. One of the workers brought a wonderful word from the Lord which broke all our hearts. The tents were erected in a field of Namaqua daisies which grow wild and in profusion.

30.9.63 Vredendal
Souls have sought the Lord and have been gloriously saved; some needing just to take the step, having been prepared by God a long while. Christians have been greatly encouraged, strengthened and blessed. Truly God has walked among us in these days. Average attendance was about 100. Among others, a whole family—father, mother and two sons of fifteen and sixteen years of age—came wonderfully through for salvation.

19.3.64 Letter from AEB headquarters
Our hearts are full of praise and gratitude to God for the way it has pleased him to use his servant, Miss Mary Morrison, during the campaigns and conventions at which she has been engaged during the past three months. Her programme

is very full, up to thirteen meetings a week, and we are concerned for her wellbeing in such a very busy programme

7.4.64 Florida Baptist Church Campaign Report from this church

Our hearts are full and our joy is running over after Miss Mary Morrison's visit. We are grateful to the Lord for her, as she came in the power of the Holy Spirit. About fifty people responded to the various appeals and sought God for various needs.

16.4.64 Welkom. Letter to AEB headquarters from the minister, Rev. D Naude:

Many, many thanks for lending us Miss Morrison. Eternity will reveal what happened here. People have been deeply moved. Ten different denominations were involved urging their people to attend. Generous offerings were donated each night. We wanted to give this to Miss Morrison but she refused to take it, asking us to send it all to you.

11.5.64 Note from headquarters

Miss Morrison's programme is very full: Pretoria Convention, Amersfoort, Dorothea Mission Birthday Conference, Primrose, Potchefstroom, East London, Port Elizabeth, Kaapmuiden Convention!

11.7.64

Mr Semark, leader of the AEB, sent a brief report of the Kaapmuiden Convention, in which he commented, 'Miss Morrison spoke from Hosea 5:15: "I will go and return to my place, till they acknowledge their offence, and seek my face." It was a mighty utterance, fearlessly outspoken and searching. A number remained behind to be dealt with.'

18.4.64–24.9.64

I was in Great Britain and Northern Ireland speaking at many meetings, most arranged by the Faith Mission. I journeyed by the Union Castle ships. This was a huge experience, and I spoke at, on average, a meeting per day throughout the period. It included the Faith Mission Edinburgh Convention as well as the Lewis convention which was taken mainly by Rev. Duncan Campbell, and where we, as a convention party, were entertained on one occasion in the Morrison home where Mary grew up. She was back from South Africa by this time and was at the house to welcome the party.

At the Edinburgh Convention, in one meeting I gave my testimony, and said, 'For any Methodists present, I came to the Lord on 24th May.' I knew that Dr Skevington Wood, the great Methodist preacher who was speaking at the convention, would pick up my reference to the date on which John Wesley received assurance of salvation in 1738. Afterwards I said, 'How did you like my apostolic succession, Dr Wood?' He answered, 'I felt my heart strangely warmed, brother,' which were the famous words Wesley used to describe his experience.

9.11.64 Fraserburg—back in South Africa
It has been a hard fight, yet six souls had definite transactions with God. The saints were greatly encouraged and blessed. Two souls of great notoriety came to Christ. May God keep them in the way for it will be a tremendous testimony if they maintain a Christian witness.

16.11.64 Carnarvon
On Saturday night we had a break with several seeking the Lord.

8.3.65 Orange Free State—on tour
It has been a great joy to visit the friends. At Steynsrus we found a woman who was so ripe that she dropped gladly into the Saviour's hands.

24.5.65 Empangeni
The mission closed on a note of real triumph as one after another testified of real blessing. On Friday night there was a real break when about half the congregation responded to the appeal. Some were Christians who came back to the Lord, and others trusted him for salvation, including a young school teacher. This is really a wonderful victory.

18.4.66 Nigel—new Protestant Annual Youth Camp
This has been a very blessed camp. There was a break on Saturday morning with about fifty seeking God, and again on Sunday morning when about eighty sought the Lord in much brokenness.

11.5.66 Florida Baptist Church Convention
This mission has been owned and blessed of God. Numbers have responded throughout the week and on Friday night there was a real break when about fifty, mostly young people, sought the Lord at the close of the meeting.

23.8.66 Port Shepstone
God has been in these meetings from the very beginning. There were over 100

on Friday night, and many Christians and a number of unsaved have sought God during the week. I have had several long conversations with numbers of the young people in groups and in homes on the subject of holiness and the fullness of the Spirit. There has been such a warmth and sympathy in the meetings and wherever we have gone on visiting. These have been great times, praise the Lord! Great times of prayer in the mornings with the saints!

8.2.67 Christiana
I have had four meetings here and in the last had the privilege of pointing six young people to the Lord. All these meetings were full of the presence of the Lord.

5.6.67
Mr Peckham has been appointed as Youth Secretary, a new post in the Band.

7.8.67 Kuruman
I had a few meetings here and rejoice in six boys who sought the Lord.

14.8.67
Miss Morrison will be available for meetings throughout the year (1968) after the Glenvar Convention in January.

5.9.67 Potchefstroom
We had the first AEB youth meeting with 250 present. Great!

19.9.67 Rossettenville Baptist Church
This has been a blessed campaign with a very real sense of the presence of the Lord. Numbers of Christians have sought the Lord in total dedication and have been richly blessed. Nine young people responded to the appeal for full-time service on Friday night.

13.11.67 Lichtenburg
God has done great and wonderful things! Thursday, Friday and Saturday were outstanding when souls were saved and cleansed. The Holy Spirit has been mightily at work and we praise him.

25.3.68 Pretoria Youth Campaign with Miss Morrison
More than 150 attended each evening and the Word was given in real power. Several were saved and quite a number met God in new ways. We hear constantly of those who have been deeply blessed. The prayer times with Mr

and Mrs MacFarlane—just the four of us—were tremendous times of power and glory! I have seldom been in such powerful prayer meetings.

Miss Morrison then went to the Potchefstroom Convention, and then on to the New Protestant youth camp in Nigel where there were 300 young folk, whereas I went to the Onrus River Easter Convention in the Cape.

2.4.68 Youth Camp and Convention Centre
We have seen and approved a piece of ground, three and a half acres, at Pennington on the Natal South Coast, fifty miles (eighty kilometres) south of Durban. (This was subsequently purchased.)

6.5.68 Krugersdorp
This short mission was blessed and one evening about twenty-five sought the Lord.

13.5.68 Johannesburg Youth Convention with Miss Morrison
Some meetings had fewer than 100 but some were up to 400. This campaign has been a great experience. The Lord was evidently in the midst and the Word came with power. On Friday night there were 430 present at the great missionary rally and about thirty responded with various needs.

3.6.68 Note from headquarters
Miss Morrison is praising the Lord for the openings in the large Dutch Reformed churches.

10.6.68 Durban Convention
There has been an unusual hunger and consciousness of God in so many of the meetings. Mr Peckham has brought the Word and there has been the powerful but quiet moving of the Holy Spirit.

23.4.68
Miss Morrison has had two busy and profitable weeks on the Witwatersrand.

30.7.68 to 5.8.68 Rhodesia—Miss Morrison
We have had thrilling reports of deep and wonderful blessing following Miss Morrison's meetings in various parts of the country including the Blantyre Keswick (Malawi). She left Rhodesia on 30.8.68 to go to Kimberley for the convention there.

4.11.68 Springs Baptist Church
The meetings were small but blessed.

Chapter 10

14.11.68 East London
Booked for three churches in the city. Miss Morrison and Mr Peckham are both in East London with full programmes.

9.12.68 Transkei
God protected Miss Eva of the YWCA, East London, and Miss Morrison from serious injury in an accident which took place in the Transkei. They were both thrown out and the car rolled down into the valley so far that when the police came to look for it, they could at first not find it. The little dog which was with them was also thrown out and merely shook himself and looked at them quizzically as if to say, 'This is not the normal way we get out of a car!'

12.4.69
Wedding Day for Mary and Colin in the Pietermaritzburg Baptist Church. The week before, he was speaking in Port Elizabeth, and she was in Warmbaths, Transvaal! People came from far and wide and it was a wonderful occasion. They have rented a home in Melville, Johannesburg, and that will be the base from which they will be working.

26.5.69 Rhodesia
Mr and Mrs Peckham drove almost immediately after their wedding to Rhodesia for four Youth Camps as well as other meetings. Their ministry in Rhodesia has been greatly blessed.

18.8.69 Kimberley Convention
The Lord has been with us with about eighty-five attending each night. Several souls were definitely saved. On Friday night eighteen people, mostly young people, responded as an indication that they were willing to go, should God call them into his service. On Saturday night, a further three souls trusted Christ for salvation. From here we go to Port Elizabeth, Cradock and the Colliesfontein Convention, Eastern Cape.

21.10.69 Pretoria Youth camp (18 miles from the city)
It was organized by the new AEB Youth Committee in Pretoria. Eighty young people attended. The Lord broke through and blessed on two wonderful occasions. A truly blessed time.

17.11.69 Johannesburg Ministers' Fraternal
Mr Peckham to give the message.

16.2.70
Miss Lynnette Schafer to go to the Peckhams in Johannesburg to help with the Youth Department.

14.5.70
Mr and Mrs Peckham have had a hectic weekend with several meetings. They now leave for a month at Pennington, Natal, to help with the project there.

10.6.70 Pennington
Work is progressing at the Pennington camp site. Mr Bill Irvine from Northern Ireland is a great help and they are working with a squad of about fifteen Africans, in preparation for the first Youth Camp which will take place at Pennington under canvas.

11.8.70 Johannesburg
Mr Peckham had great liberty in preaching God's Word in the youth meeting.

11.8.70 Appointment:
Mr Peckham is appointed vice-principal of Glenvar Bible College, under Mr Pienaar the principal. He remains Youth Leader. They will take up their abode in the flat in the College.

12.8.70
Colin Morris Peckham born in Johannesburg!

25.8.70 Johannesburg Quarterly Youth Meeting
We had over 100 in this meeting and it was a very good time indeed. Had a great time in the Florida Baptist Church on Friday night.

9.11.70 Youth Challenge Magazine
This is run off on our kitchen table. We are printing over 1,000 in Afrikaans and the same in English. Lynette is enjoying the work and is giving herself to it with all her heart.

11–13.12.70
The first Youth Camp on Bok Rossouw's farm outside Bothaville, Orange Free State. This was a great time with about 150 young people.

December 1970
Journeyed in a Volkswagen Beetle all the way to Cape Town, via

Pietermaritzburg and East London. We are now sorting ourselves out in the flat above the entrance at the College.

4.8.71
Heather Ann Peckham born in Cape Town!

29.4.74
Christine Mary Peckham born in Cape Town!

**AEB Kaapmuiden convention
in the Transvaal**

Camps and conventions

While holding missions is the main work of the AEB, conventions are its life-blood. Today there are permanent camp centres, but when I was involved, the camps consisted of tents on farms to which families came and stayed for the long weekend, attending all the meetings. These have always been times of tremendous blessing.

My first convention was the Easter Flora Convention. Tents were transported to a farm near Flora in the eastern Orange Free State. Koos and I, with the help of a few others, pitched numbers of tents under the spreading branches of large pine trees. There were probably only about sixty people camping there for the long weekend, but what a time we had! The heavy rain did not deter the people from seeking God. There were some memorable meetings when God broke through. I remember two high school girls sitting at the back of the tent sobbing their hearts out. Together with many others, they met God that morning. One of them later became the wife of a superintendent in the AEB. When the other went back to school she witnessed fearlessly for the Lord, and through her witness twenty-five high school young people came to Christ. A Christian teacher in that school said to me a year later, 'She has left the school now, but I still have ten of her converts in my class!'

That year Koos and I went to the Kaapmuiden Convention in the Eastern Transvaal. This convention had been established about twenty-five years before and was now recognized all over the country as a special place of great spiritual blessing. There were about 800 or more people under canvas on the farm of Laurie Wiid. The kitchen consisted of huge black cooking pots in the open. They consumed an ox a day, and an ox and a half a day over the weekend. The leader of the convention said to us in his opening remarks, 'Don't go swimming; there are crocodiles!' People came with great

Chapter 11

expectancy. For the workers, the times of prayer together in the mornings were the cream of the convention. How God met with us! Old Mr H T de Villiers gave the morning Bible readings. They were mighty! The presence of God was everywhere. One morning virtually the whole convention sought God in much brokenness. Before, if they had knelt to pray, they would carefully place a handkerchief or something on the ground to kneel on, but that morning they did not bother about handkerchiefs. They simply fell on that red soil and wept their way to the Cross. What mighty moments they were. Lives were changed for ever. I was asked to lead the singing at the convention and I led it with great gusto, attempting at times to make a 'choir' of the convention. That set me apart in my special expertise as a song leader, for the large AEB meetings all over, for all the years that I was in the AEB.

SNAKE IN THE NIGHT

To set up the convention, Koos, Rassie Venter and I drove a three-ton lorry loaded with tents and equipment from Pretoria to the farm, a distance of about 240 miles (400 kilometres). The ground had been cleared somewhat and, with about fifteen Africans, we began to pitch the tents. At the end of the first day about sixty were standing. We slept in a small marquee together. At about midnight, I awoke to find a snake gliding over my neck! I hurled it—where, I knew not—and screamed! I did not know that such ghastly sounds could ever come out of my mouth. I leapt to the tent-pole and climbed, screaming! These poor fellows! They awoke to these terrible earth-shattering screams. I was terrified. Koos grabbed his torch. I jumped onto Rassie's bed, for I did not want my feet to touch the floor.

'What's the matter?' shouted Koos.

I bared my neck and cried out in desperation, 'There was a snake around my neck! Am I bitten? Am I bitten?'

Koos shone the torch around my neck and said, 'No, you're all right, but where's the snake?'

With that, he walked outside to look for the snake—leaving us in the dark! He returned and Rassie said with quivering voice, 'Er, er, wwwhich, which way did you throw it?'

'I don't know!' I exclaimed.

Koos stood there with the torch in his hand on his thigh and said, 'It's the devil, man!' meaning that it was an attack from Satan. 'Come, let's pray.'

He prayed briefly, and Rassie admitted later, 'I kept my eyes wide open when Koos prayed!'

Koos looked at me and said, 'Now brother, have faith. Get into bed.'

'No! No!' I said vehemently, 'Faith and works! We must search this tent first!' We carefully looked all over the tent, but the snake was nowhere to be found. I am sure that it got a bigger fright than I did and vanished into the night as fast as it could slither!

The next morning I was working with my penknife and I put it back into my pocket, forgetting that there was a hole in my pocket. It slid down my leg. I froze and nearly had a fit as I grabbed at my leg, only realizing a moment later that it was not another snake, but merely my penknife. For the next three weeks when my coat collar touched my neck, I would react with a sudden involuntary grab at my neck, thinking subconsciously that it was another reptile attack! Truly it was a case of 'Death at my shoulder,' but I survived, praise the Lord!

After the convention we packed the lorry and stayed with some friends for a few days' rest before returning to Pretoria. We set out at 4.00am and, about an hour later while climbing the long mountain to get out of the low veldt, the lorry's engine gave in and we came to an abrupt halt. It was dark with only the moonlight to guide us. Koos stuck his head into the engine compartment to see what he could do, Rassie walked around in a great overcoat, as it was quite cold, and I decided that I would like to know the length of the white lines in the middle of the road, so I lay down on one of them to estimate its length! At that moment an African came pushing his bicycle up the hill. He must have thought this to be a queer lot, one with his legs sticking out of the engine, another wandering aimlessly around dressed for the arctic and a third person lying on the ground! He gave us a wide berth, walking as far from us as he could, but as he drew abreast of me, I leapt up and called to him in Zulu. He simply vanished, and ran for his life, overcome, I am sure, with terror! Rassie hitched a lift to Pretoria, got the necessary part and returned for Koos to repair the engine. We were once again in business and on our way.

The Kroonstad Convention was held on the banks of the river that ran through the city. We pitched the tents and the convention was in full swing when a thunderstorm struck upstream in the river's catchments area. In the middle of the night the tents which were closest to the river had to be vacated in a hurry! There was no time to save the large meeting tent and it was simply swept away. The next morning the superintendent was a picture of misery as he surveyed the wreckage when a retired pilgrim came upon the scene. She was her own buoyant self and laughed at his serious face. 'Don't worry,' she said happily, 'now you'll get new tents!' And so it turned out to be. God moved in the hearts of Christians who heard about the tragedy, and, lo and behold, it was soon possible to order beautiful new tents which were well used in the service of the Lord.

OTHER CONVENTIONS

Many stories could be told of the conventions which took place all over South Africa. We were at Onrus River Convention about eighty miles (130 kilometres) from Cape Town. I was only a young worker but was given two opportunities to speak, right at the beginning, and at the 9.00am Sunday morning meeting. The first meeting passed without anything wonderful to report, but on the Saturday night I crept out of my tent and sought God from the early hours, for I was greatly burdened for this meeting. I had a strong impression from God that there would be a break at this early morning meeting. I went to the meeting knowing that God would work in power—and he did! People were broken in his presence and tears flowed as they knelt at the front or just where they were at the close of the meeting. I went to have a cup of tea but there were few people there. They were all seeking God in their tents or in the main tent. I walked past the tent of the main speaker, Mr Pienaar, as he emerged. He had heard all about the break, and he grabbed me by the arm. 'What am I to say now?' he said. 'Just what God tells you to say, sir,' I said. He went to the tent and preached a great gospel message, showing what the workers were preaching when they went out on their missions. It was a great day and we gave God the glory.

We held a convention in The Kloof, Rustenburg, Transvaal. I was to speak on Friday night at the young people's meeting. God helped me in a wonderful way and the Word came with a great deal of liberty. I made an appeal and while I was still speaking, the people began to come to the front. I did not ask them to kneel, but they did—about 100 of them. They knelt on the mat at the front and in the aisles. The superintendent took over and I moved to the side against the tent wall. My wife stood beside me, took my hand and whispered to me as I stood weeping, 'This is God's minute!'

Those youngsters sought God that night and found him abundantly able to meet their need.

We were again at the Easter Onrus River camp convention. We were all under canvas. There were about 500 people in the large tent on that last Monday. Mary, my wife, was to speak at 9.00am, I was to speak at 11am and after dinner Danie Drotskie was to close the convention at 2.00pm Mary and I climbed into our little Volkswagen Beetle at about 8.20am to pray. In her prayer she quoted Isaiah 63:1 'Who is this that cometh from Edom, with dyed garments from Bozrah, this that is glorious in his apparel, travelling in the greatness of his strength? I that speak in righteousness, mighty to save.' She pictured the heavenly choirs calling to one another, 'Who, who is this? He is coming from the land of the enemy, from Edom; from the earth to heaven. Who can it be? He must be a king; look at his glorious apparel. He must be victorious for he is travelling in the greatness of his strength. But he has been in a fight; he's wounded, for his garments are dyed! Who, who can it be? "I that speak in righteousness, mighty to save."' Oh, with the eye of faith we saw Jesus! We broke before him in that car. What a time we had! From there we walked across the grass to the tent, filled with expectant, prayerful people. As the Word came, what power! What unction! I looked up and more than half of the congregation were sitting sobbing silently in their seats. When she closed, a well-respected middle-aged teacher ran to the front and fell on his knees. He wept as though his heart would break. But he was not the only one. At the front and all over the tent people broke before the Lord and sought him as they poured out their hearts with many tears. There was a great weeping in the presence of the Lord. The presence of God filled the place. What a morning! Years later we were still hearing of people who met with God that morning. It was surely one of the most powerful meetings I have ever been in. One can only say that God walked among us and men and women, boys and girls bent before him in deep humility and brokenness.

At Magudu in Zululand, tents were pitched and about seventy people came. It was hot! The sun blazed down on that meeting tent. We lifted the sides but there was no breeze to ease the stifling conditions. Mr Semark, the leader of the AEB, gave the morning Bible readings. He spoke about the gates of Jerusalem—the water gate, the sheep gate, and so on. People were praying, but in these conditions, what could happen? One morning in the heat, he droned on and on about the gates. I watched from the back as people tried their utmost to keep awake. They rubbed their eyes and moved their positions, but it was oh so hot! I said to myself, 'Please Mr Semark, say "Amen" and allow these people to escape from this torture.' At last he came to an end and I breathed a sigh of relief. Now the poor people could escape. But no, the leader of the meeting, Mr Harmse, said, 'Maybe God has spoken to you this morning and you might want to seek him.' Oh, no, is he going to prolong the meeting? 'We'll sing a song,' he said, 'and if you want to seek God feel free to come to the front and pray.' The people turned sleepily to their hymn books, and sang—sleepily! Then, suddenly, it happened! God fell upon the meeting. Suddenly he came to his temple. Suddenly, in the middle of the hymn, we were simply enveloped by the presence of the Lord. God stepped in! The people broke before God and sought him everywhere in that tent. I sat at the back with my head in my hands and wept! The tears streamed from my eyes. God took the field. I was so grateful that I had not been leading the meeting that day! It was a day long to be remembered by all who were there.

There is such a mystery in the coming of the presence of God to a meeting, but when he comes, it is unforgettable. Those moments of God are so, so precious. They are life-transforming. When you have been in the presence of God like that, for ever after, you know what you want, and you are never satisfied with anything less.

We pitched tents near to Springbok in Namaqualand for a small convention. Danie Drotskie was with us and tells of the moment that he approached the tent when I was speaking. He says that as he came to within sixty yards of the tent, suddenly he was conscious of an overwhelming sense of God's presence. 'I still get goose pimples when I think of it,' he said. God was working in a wonderful way at the camp. But one of the workers brought a word from Philippians chapter 1 and was greatly used. God simply broke through and people sought him with all their hearts in the tent and outside. It was mighty!

We had had a half-night of prayer at this convention, and during this prayer-time, one man indicated his need in his prayer. I took him aside after the meeting—it must have been about midnight—and asked if I could help him. He said 'I have come 160 miles (260 kilometres) in an old car that does just nine miles to a tin (he meant a gallon) over bad roads to this convention with one desire, that is, to be filled with the Holy Ghost.' We went aside in the moonlight and knelt beside a large bush (there are no trees in this arid area), and sought God. There he yielded himself fully to God and trusted the Lord to take control of his life, to cleanse him from sin, and to fill him with the Holy Spirit. Three years later we were working along the Orange River where there are many small farms under irrigation, making it a highly productive area. We went to see this very man with whom I had prayed at the camp. He said, 'Get into my car and I will introduce you to some people.' He took us to one and another up and down the river. 'This one I led to the Lord three months ago, and this one I led to the Lord a year ago, this one came through nine months ago,' he said as he drove us around. Amazing! 'And it all began when I prayed with you under that bush in the moonlight!' he said.

We were on the farmyard in farm buildings, in the homestead and in tents for the Colliesfontein Convention in the Eastern Cape. One day there was a mighty word from the Lord. We were spellbound. God came to that meeting in a powerful way. Danie D. was leading the meeting, and when he rose, it was obvious that he was greatly moved. He said, 'I have never been in such a meeting in all my life.' People took the opportunity and prayed in the tent and in their rooms. Afterwards when we queued for the meal, the people gave Mary a wide berth. They seemed to think that she had come from Mars or some place, for she had been clothed with the powerful presence of the Lord. She had been used earlier on the islands of North Uist and Tiree in revival blessing. She knew the secret of finding the Lord's presence and on this occasion was wonderfully used. (The revival in North Uist in 1957/58 is recorded by one of the converts, Rev. John Ferguson, *When God came down.*)

Colin conducting the AEB choir

Youthwork

I had completed nearly eight years of hard mission work, and now I was appointed Youth Leader of the Mission. For this I needed a car. I was working in the Western Transvaal and one day I attended a church in Potchefstroom. An elderly gentleman whom I knew quite well invited me to his home after the morning service. As a hobby he did leatherwork and he wanted to show me his work. At the end of the visit he put a leather car key-case in my hand. I thanked him and it burned in my pocket all the way to the headquarters. I placed it on my bed and got down on my knees at the bedside. 'Lord,' I said, 'I've got the button, now give me the coat! I've got the key ring, I now need a car!' One day a man came to me, placed the keys of a car in my hand, and said, 'Go, and seek souls for Jesus.' The car had come. It was a red Volkswagen Beetle and it carried me all over the land in the service of the King.

SILVER AND GOLD FOR THE HOUSE OF GOD

As I left the Council meeting in which I was appointed Youth Leader, I said to the matron, Mrs Kellerman, 'We are going to need thousands of rands to build a youth centre.' I had it in my heart. Before I took up the position I was still working missions and at that particular time I was holding a mission in Kuruman, almost in the Kalahari Desert. God was speaking to my heart and I drew all sorts of buildings to scale for the new camp site! How on earth would I be able to find funds for the project, and where would it be built? Suddenly God spoke to me from Ezra 7:15–16: 'Carry the silver and gold ... for the house of their God.' 'Bestow it out of the king's treasure house' (v. 20). Oh, my! God spoke it right into my heart.

I placed the matter on the AEB's Council Agenda. The Council met in Cape Town, about twenty-five of them, from all over the country. At last my request was on the table. 'Mr Peckham wants to buy or build a youth camp and convention centre on the Natal South Coast.' Nothing like this had ever been contemplated in the history of the AEB. They were content with tents, but I felt that the days of tents were past and we should move into permanent buildings. I was a junior member of the Council and I expected to be strongly opposed. After all, who was I that I should propose such a major project? I examined the carpet at my feet, it seemed for years, waiting for the explosion. It was, oh, such a long, long silence. Then the chairman simply said, 'Well, brother, if you have the money, go ahead. Next item on the agenda.' I couldn't believe my ears! It was through without a fight! There was no battle! The chairman thought that he was safe for he knew that I had no money, and I knew that I was safe for I had the promises of God! I left the Council meeting walking on air. I was ecstatic!

PENNINGTON

I returned to Bloemfontein where I had a room in the Orange Free State headquarters. with Koos and Ina Engelbrecht, my former co-worker. From there I attempted to find a suitable, affordable property almost 400 miles (660 kilometres) away. The search for a property began. On 29th March, 1968, I went to view three acres of land at Pennington, fifty miles (eighty kilometres) south of Durban. It was a beautiful piece of ground but too expensive. Did the gentleman know of any other property for sale? Yes he did, three acres on the hill about four hundred yards away. I drove on to this property, forced my way through the dense undergrowth and subtropical forest. I was thrilled with the possibilities and knelt at the foot of a large tree. I had walked on a number of properties but never had I had the witness that I now had in connection with this piece of ground. I prayed out loud, 'Lord, give us this property!' That very morning in my quiet time God had given me Exodus 14:13–15: 'Fear ye not, stand still, and see the salvation of the LORD, which he will show you this day.' Even though I had not seen the agent, and did not know the price, I had an overwhelming conviction that this was of God. I later saw the agent and discovered that the price was R8,500 of which R4,000 had to be paid when the deeds were signed.

When I was in the Transvaal, someone who had heard that there might be a development on the Natal south coast gave me R500. Over the few months this had increased to R1,000. On a journey I stayed with someone overnight. She had heard of the possibility of a centre being built, and at the breakfast table handed me a cheque for R3,000! So we had the R4,000 and the deeds were signed. The property was ours! A farmer phoned Mr Harmse, the Natal District Superintendent, and said that he had sold his farm and was sending him R3,500 for the Centre. The AEB was now the possessor of a valuable piece of land on the Natal south coast paid for in record time!

And the buildings? I was in Potchefstroom when a young couple phoned and asked to see me. 'We have a plot of ground which we are selling. If it reaches R1,000 we will give that money to this project,' they said. It did and they handed me a cheque for R1,000. It was a sacrificial gift. 'There goes your car, Mummy,' he said. 'That's quite all right,' she replied. 'It's for the Lord.' Wouter wept, Elsie wept, I wept. With this precious R1,000 gift the buildings were begun.

I brought my newly-wed bride to the place and we worked there physically for the month of May, 1969. Bill Irvine from Northern Ireland offered his services and he stayed on the grounds heading up the whole project for three years. With the help of labourers and skilled men, too, he transferred what was on paper to actual buildings. The Youth Camp and Convention Centre stood! That which had been conceived in Kuruman was born in Pennington. The first camp convention was held 7-12 July, 1970, with Rev. Maynard James from Britain. About 170 attended the dedication service on Saturday 11th. It was a good camp with souls saved, blessed and called of God. My diary records, 'First harvest of the vision.' Since then many souls have been saved and mightily blessed on these camp grounds. And when the AEB saw that it worked, other convention centres sprang up all over the country so that there are now seven AEB camp centres in Southern Africa. Praise the Lord!

OTHER ASPECTS OF YOUTH MINISTRY

Youth Camps! We began from where I had been working last, in the Western Transvaal. Bok and Grietha Rossouw were farming in the Bothaville area in the Orange Free State, not too far from Potchefstroom, Western Transvaal, and they invited us to hold a youth camp on their farm, 11th–14th December 1970. It was tremendous! We left Potchefstroom with several vehicles filled with young people. Others come from places where I had recently worked campaigns and elsewhere, and the camp was up and running. There were about 150 young folk there. We had three speakers and we took turns. God was greatly glorified as these young folk sought God throughout the few days that we were there. For a few years this became an annual event.

On one occasion, one of the pilgrims gave a mighty word on Mary and the broken cruise of oil. The whole camp was broken and those young people sought the Lord with all their hearts. I took about eight of the lads outside to pray with them. As I did so I passed Hannetjie, one of the workers, with about ten girls gathered around her. They were sobbing their eyes out. I thought, 'What a beautiful nest.' Having dealt with my boys I returned to see if I could help anyone else. There was no-one in the tent except Hannetjie. She looked at me and said with intense emotion, 'Colin, God has come!' Yes, we all knew that!

At another of these Bothaville camps, there had been good teaching and the meetings were inspirational but there had just been no break which we knew should come. We, as workers, prayed into the night, but there was no break. I was speaking at the last meeting on the Sunday afternoon when the parents of many of the young folk had come to fetch their children. I was speaking on prayer, Bible reading and witnessing to help them on their way after the camp, when I sensed God coming into the meeting. I turned the message to bring the challenge of dedication. The atmosphere was filled with the presence of the Lord and when I made the briefest of appeals, virtually the whole camp responded. There were many tears as they sought God. It was a great break as God took over the meeting and many souls found new deliverance in the Lord Jesus. It was also satisfying in that it happened when the parents were there so that they, too, could be blessed and could see what was actually happening at these camps. In fact I cannot remember a camp which we held in all those years, where God did not break through in mighty blessing. We give praise to him for his wonderful presence, Revealing himself to those who were there, breaking hearts and building them up again in a spirit of dedication and praise.

At one youth camp held in a predominantly Afrikaans area, I felt that I could not use Mary as she was not able to communicate in their language and they would not understand English too well. She said one day, 'I have a message for these young people.' I was caught in the horns of a dilemma. What was I to do? Should I put her on and risk their not grasping what she was saying, or should I keep her from the platform? I decided that I could not chance it. 'What is it that the Lord has put on your heart?' I asked.

'I was afraid, because I was naked; and I hid myself,' (Genesis 3:10) she replied. I did not put her on the platform.

When the young people gave their testimonies at the end of the camp, about five of them said, 'God spoke to me through a verse in Genesis, "I was afraid, because I was naked and I hid myself"!' Had Mary spoken, I am sure that that meeting would have been the great blessing of the camp. I made a mistake.

We spoke at various church youth camps, and organized our own camps and youth conventions across the country. It was a time of great blessing, but all too short as we were soon to embark upon another chapter in our lives.

**Colin and Mary on an outing to
Portobello near Edinburgh, 1964**

Mary and marriage

I heard of Mary's ministry in the Highlands and Islands of Scotland and in the Midlands of England from Rev. Duncan Campbell and I was praying for her before I met her. We met briefly in Cape Town in January, 1964, and when I went to Great Britain later that year, we met in her home on the Isle of Lewis with the convention party. We were together with all the other pilgrims of the Faith Mission for the Edinburgh Convention in August and we struck up a friendship. I went back to South Africa and we continued corresponding. I felt that if I was not going to continue with this friendship, it would not be fair to her and I should no longer continue with the correspondence. I told her that I would write no more letters, and with that she took my twenty-two letters, which really consisted of mission reports and theological perspectives, and threw them in the bin! So all my theology was lost, and that was the end of our relationship!

But she was invited to South Africa for a year's ministry in 1968, so we met again. She spoke at the large Annual Glenvar Convention in Cape Town at the beginning of the year and then was booked up all over the country for the year ahead. I booked her for a few youth campaigns in various places. In fact we were together quite a lot throughout the year. She knew in her heart that we would be married but neither spoke a word nor gave a hint, suffering in silence my seeming indifference to the matter. In fact I was in a turmoil. How could I give my life to a woman when God was beginning to use me here and there, and when I would be all over the country in ministry? If I were to marry Mary Morrison, I would simply be carrying her bags around as she conducted her itinerant ministry! No! It would never work! And yet—was this of God? We were in several places together for ministry and carefully avoided each other, other than being on the platform together at the meetings. Unless I knew that she was to be my wife I did not feel that I could make any advance towards her. It would not be fair to her for I simply could not pick her up and then drop her ignominiously some time later. My battle was with the Lord. Was she to be my wife or not? If God did not point me in her direction I could not move. She suffered greatly and lost thirty pounds in weight during the year!

TYPEWRITER

I was, at the time, organizing youth meetings all over and she spoke at the Pretoria Youth Convention. The youth work was just beginning and I needed a long-carriage typewriter. I went to Selwyn Kettles, the Pretoria Christian bookshop manager, and asked if he had contacts for a typewriter. Yes, he did have, and we drove to the business site to see the typewriters. I chose one and the man said, 'That is R180.'

'What about business discount?' asked Selwyn.

'All right, I'll give it to you for R120,' he said.

'And what about cash discount?' persisted Selwyn.

'Oh sir!' the man exclaimed. 'OK, I'll give it to you for R117.'

'Three rand is three rand,' said Selwyn, commenting on the saving that had been made.

I did not have any money, so Selwyn paid the bill. I would reimburse him when I had money in the youth department. We drove away. I dropped him at his shop and went to pick up Mary Morrison to take her to the people with whom I was staying, as they had invited her for lunch that day. As we drove, she leant down to her bag and drew out something, laying it on my lap. I looked down and there was a roll of banknotes. 'Oh no,' I said, 'I am trusting the Lord for all my upkeep and so are you. I am not taking any money from you, Mary Morrison. You need every penny.' I put it on her lap.

'But the Lord told me to give it to you,' she said, and put it back on my lap.

'No! No!' I said, 'This is what God has given you, and you need it.' I placed it again on her lap.

She placed it on my lap again and said, 'I don't know why I should give you this money. It's a strange amount. It's R117!'

I drew the car to the side of the road and gaped at her. I pulled the paperwork from my pocket and said, 'Do you see that?' Then I pointed to the typewriter on the back seat, and said, 'Do you see that?' That was bought for R117 just half an hour ago!' Whew! The Lord took our breath away!

PRETORIA MINISTRY

Very good numbers attended the Pretoria Youth Week. Of course the leader and the preacher would have to pray together, but how were we to do so? We were simply two young people, and it would not be proper for us to get alone somewhere to pray each day. As we left the meeting that first night, Mary spotted Mr and Mrs MacFarlane who had been ministering in Canada. She grabbed his arm. 'Uncle Mac, come and pray with us in the mornings,' she said.

'With pleasure,' he replied. So we gathered in a home each morning and prayed through until lunch time. What mighty times of prayer they were! I can still hear Uncle Mac storming the gates of glory for an hour or an hour and a half each day. We were caught up in the sheer power of the exercise. Even today I recall with a tear in my eye the glory of those mornings as we trod the forecourts of heaven. What a wonderful privilege to be with those who knew how to pray and who were able to come to the side of those in the forefront of the battle!

I drove Mary back to the home where she was staying in Pretoria each night after the meeting, and on the way we stopped at an open-air cafe in Arcadia. There we slowly sipped cool drinks or milkshakes, and that was about the only courtship that we ever had! There was no close contact and I was still very unsure of what I should do with regard to Mary Morrison.

She was booked for a few campaigns in Rhodesia (now Zimbabwe), with the AEB and journeyed north for these meetings, determined not to take any remuneration from the AEB as she knew that they had financial difficulties. God greatly blessed her ministry across the country. In fact in Fort Victoria a number of folk came to the Lord and a church was begun from that campaign and it subsequently joined the Anglican Communion. On her return she was to go first to Bulawayo before returning to South Africa. Albert Brandt, the superintendent, insisted, 'If you won't take any money for all your services here, please let me pay for your ticket back to South Africa.'

'Well,' she said, 'if I do not have enough when I go to buy the ticket, I'll come to you.' She bought toiletries, and small items on the station, then queued for her ticket. She paid for it and had one brown coin left over!

'How much do you need?' asked Albert.

'No, I am quite all right,' she replied and hopped on to the train to begin her long journey. The people with whom she stayed overnight in Bulawayo gave her £20 and R19 (South African currency) when she left, and that was almost the total amount that anyone was allowed to take out of the country!

SHOULD I MARRY MARY?

The Christmas of 1968 was miserable. I stayed with my parents in Pietermaritzburg and was in prayer most of the time. Should I marry Mary? Is this the will of God? Oh, why is this issue not simple and plain? I desired to do the will of God so earnestly that my very earnestness almost deviated me from it! I was more and more convinced that I should go ahead and pop the question. I travelled by car to Cape Town, a journey of 1,000 miles (1,600 kilometres) via the Transkei, which meant I would be passing through East London where Mary was staying at the YWCA. I called on my friend, the Rev. Rex Mathie, who was a minister in East London, and in the conversation I said, 'What do you think of that girl Mary Morrison?' He swung on his heel and pointed straight at me.

'You should marry that girl,' he said. 'When you were both on the platform here a little while back, I said to myself, "These two are already married in spirit." You can't go wrong, brother!'

'I will!' I said, and that night I drove Mary to a beautiful spot overlooking the sea and proposed. She accepted and we drove back. It was midnight and it was the first of January. The cars were hooting and the fireworks lit the sky as we journeyed into the new year together.

If only that were the end of the conflict. The next morning I woke to the horror of what I had done! I had gone out of the will of God! How could God ever use me again? My life was now in tatters! What could I do to escape? Nothing! I had ruined my life and there was no getting out of the fix I was now in! Woe is me!

Poor Mary! She endured my traumas with gracious calmness.

She was again to be involved in the Annual Glenvar Convention in Cape Town so we drove to Cape Town together. I was in total misery. Eventually some light shone on my pathway and I wrote a letter to the chairman of the AEB asking permission to marry Mary and for us to remain in the work as a married couple. This was just the courteous thing to do in a mission situation. No-one knew about our relationship. I sat in the Council meeting immediately after the convention, and eventually Mr Pienaar, the chairman, took my letter and actually stood up to read it. I fled from the room. The dye was cast! Mary was just down the passage and I said to her, 'Mr Pienaar is about to read my letter!'

'Would you like me to go with you?' she asked calmly.

'Yes,' I said, and we walked to the glass door of the room where the Council was sitting. We were seen through the door and Mr Pienaar called us both in. We sat together, under the quizzical looks of the Council members. He said, 'I have something to read to you all which I am sure is most certainly in the will of God.' The letter was read. Next to me sat Selwyn Kettles who gaped at me wide-eyed. 'Are you sure?' he gasped under his breath.

'Yes!' I answered emphatically, trying to convince myself! So we began, with my many fears but eventually with the consciousness that God had put us together for his purposes in grace. What we were doing separately we would now do together and the Lord blessed us as we laboured in his vineyard. We never had a day's adjustment and our lives simply flowed together in the service of the King.

Interestingly, she had received honorariums throughout her ministry during 1968, but had given all the money away to the work of God, so that when we were engaged, she had only fifty pence to her name. I married her for her money!

At several of the places where she or I had worked the folk arranged for us to come for a kitchen tea, or a Tupperware party, or a linen shower, or, at some places it was simply a full-blown reception! Gifts were given at these places and when we set up home we did not need to buy a single item for the home. Linen, towels and a host of things were freely given. God marvellously provided through so many people who had been blessed across the land.

WEDDING BELLS

The wedding took place in my home church, the Pietermaritzburg Baptist Church. It was a wonderful event. Mary travelled down from the Transvaal where she had been ministering and I from Port Elizabeth where I had been ministering. Mary was given a wedding gown by the folk in Bulawayo, and the church rallied to produce the reception held in the church hall. Mary, having got dressed at the YWCA, was given away by her kilted brother-in-law from Pretoria. For the sake of those who travelled so many miles across the country to be there, we had our photos taken before the wedding so that we were able to simply drive around the block from the church and come in almost immediately to the reception accompanied by the bagpipes! We cut the cake which was decorated with heather and proteas, the flowers of our two countries. Marjorie Eva, from East London, who had so much to do with the wedding, took a tier of the decorated cake, well protected in a firm box and addressed to Mary's mother. This she gave to an officer on board a ship bound for the UK and asked him to post it when the ship docked in England. The Morrisons, on the Isle of Lewis, received it without one thing broken.

From the wedding we drove to a motel high in the Drakensburg mountains on our way to Johannesburg where we had a flat, or rather the top half of a house. The owner had said to me some time back, 'You're going to get married, and when you do, I've got a house for you.' (She saw what was happening before I did!) Flats and houses were very difficult to find at that time in Johannesburg, but God went before and provided a home for us through this good lady. We began our married life with borrowed beds, (one four inches higher than the other) tied together with wire, bare boards (no carpets), and boxes of books! Someone later gave us a settee and two easy chairs. We had to rid the settee of mice which had made their abode there when it was stored in the man's garage.

Three days after the wedding we were on our way to Rhodesia to hold four youth camps. We arrived at the famous Beit Bridge across the Zambezi River and the procedures took so long that it was almost night before we got across. We would find a place to sleep on the other side—but no, there was no room anywhere. Where should we go? 'To the Lion and Elephant,' we were told.

'Where is that?' we asked.

'About sixty miles (a hundred kilometres) north.' So in the dark on the narrow strip roads we ventured into this new land. As there was no mains power, the generator had already been switched off when we arrived and the lights were out, but we were welcomed to a rondavel (a round hut). We put the candles out, got into bed—but began to scratch. Then we heard a strange 'shushing' sound. What on earth was this? We shone the torch on the walls and about half of the walls were covered in ants! The walls in fact looked as if they had been painted white above and brown on the bottom half. And the ants were in bed with us! I quickly called those in charge and an African was sent in with a pump to squirt insecticide all over the walls and floor while the bride sat curled up at the top of the bed in her pretty nightdress! He swept the ants away and then disappeared. Oh, how we laughed! We survived!

The youth camps were small but tremendous. At every one of them, God broke through and we were able to counsel earnest young people, many of whom were broken and in tears. They were thrilled with the camps. Between the camps we had a few days off. During one of these times we went to a wild animal farm near Fort Victoria and watched the cheetahs having a meal behind fencing in the back yard. 'I take them for a walk like dogs every day,' said the owner, 'and sometimes they climb over this high fence, come into the kitchen and rub themselves against my wife's legs!' He had a lion which he had reared since it was a cub. It was called Dandy or Dandy-lion! He called it and it came running. It rubbed itself like a cat against the mesh wire. Mary put her hand through the wire and stroked the lion from the beginning of its mane to the tip of its tail. It turned and rubbed itself again and Mary stroked it again. I was horrified. 'Mary,' I said, 'if he turns around, in one snap, your hand is gone!'

'Oh, he's so lovely,' she replied.

During another interval between camps we went to the Victoria Falls. This fantastic sight has to be seen to be believed. Water a mile wide falls 365 feet (over 100 metres) into a crack in the flat earth. When we were there the water was almost at the highest level it had ever been. The spray can sometimes be seen for miles around. Rainbows large and small dance around everywhere. You cannot keep dry—the spray drenches you. We went to see the lunar rainbow at night. It was an eerie white bow hanging over the falls. What an experience!

Eventually we returned to Johannesburg, to the flat in Melville where we set up home and began our life's work together.

Constantia principal's home

Johannesburg and then Cape Town

We soon realized that we needed to keep in touch with all these young people so the letter which I had been sending out became a magazine run off on our kitchen table. We called it *Youth Challenged*. It developed and its numbers increased. We sent it out in Afrikaans and also in English. Later Lynnette Schafer came to stay with us and did sterling work on the little magazine. Later still at the Bible College in Cape Town, we continued publishing it in a press which the Lord gave us. This press operated in our double garage in Cape Town until it outgrew that, and other premises had to be found for it. At its height we were producing 12,000 copies every two months. They were all free and the Lord supplied all the need! The magazine was a source of great blessing to the young folk all over the country, and built up the youth work throughout the land.

From Johannesburg we launched our work among young people, in churches, and in the organization of our own camps in various places across the country.

On one occasion we were booked to speak at a camp near Parys, eighty miles (130 kilometres) away. Our little Volkswagen Beetle broke down at the most awkward time. We took it to the garage and found it to be a major job, which the garage completed in record time, but we could not take the car from the garage unless we paid for it. The price was R441, money which we did not have. We cried to the Lord to come to our rescue! Mary went to the post office the day before we had to leave for the camp and opened the post from the box. She was so thrilled that she phoned me from the post office, not even waiting to get home. 'There is a cheque for R450!' she exclaimed excitedly. No-one had known about the need. The car was retrieved and off we went.

Chapter 14

PREGNANCY AND CHILDBIRTH

On the way to a camp in the Orange Free State we passed the home of some friends who showed us a beautiful pram which they were giving us. We were a little taken aback, for months had passed since our wedding and it seemed that no baby was on the way, so we did not know what to say. On our way back from the camp we called there but by this time we were sure that Mary was pregnant. So we loaded the pram on to the roof of our car and off we went to Johannesburg with joyous possibilities in the car and on its roof!

Mary had very good care throughout the pregnancy from one of South Africa's senior gynaecologists. The time eventually came and I drove her to the hospital at 8.00pm on 11th August, 1970. She was thirty-seven years old and the doctor was summoned. He arrived at 9.00pm and gave orders for an immediate caesarean section to be done. The nurses put on the drips and made preparations. I said, 'Can you not give her an injection, doctor?'

'Yes,' he said, 'but that won't do her much good.'

I went in to Mary and said to her, 'What shall we do?'

'I am in no condition to make any decision,' she gasped between contractions. 'You must decide.' Oh, woe is me—I had to decide!

'Doctor,' I said, 'I think that we will have a normal birth.'

'If this were my wife, I would have a section,' he replied. 'You are committing her to a night of hell. At this age, the labour will not be shorter than sixteen to twenty hours. I'll see you in the morning.' With that he left the hospital while angry nurses took the drips out. How could anyone oppose Dr Bletcher?

I lay on a bench downstairs, and had ten babies! Just after midnight, I heard some sounds outside and went out to find Dr Bletcher getting into the lift. I jumped in with him and he said with great surprise, 'The baby is coming!'

I said, 'Doctor we are so grateful for all your care of Mary over this whole period, but we are Christians, and God gave us a word from the book of Isaiah at the beginning of this pregnancy. It is, "I have made, and I will bear; even I will carry, and will deliver you" (Isaiah 46:4). When you said that you would cut, I had to decide between your word and God's Word, and I chose to believe God.' The lift opened and he went through and delivered our firstborn, whereupon, Mary told him the same story and gave him the same verse! A few months later, one of our lady workers went to see him about some complaint and he asked about Mary, saying that he had never seen anything like that in all his experience, for all women having their first baby at that age always had extremely long periods of labour. 'Who is that fellow who knows more about obstetrics than I do?' he asked, 'Oh yes, Isaiah!' It was a great testimony and we rejoiced.

The Florida Baptist Church decorated a wonderful cradle and gave us everything we needed for the new arrival. Baby Colin Morris was the eleventh baby in that cradle.

UNIVERSITY STUDIES

I had begun studying with the University of South Africa (UNISA) in nearby Pretoria, as well as with the Baptist Theological College in Johannesburg, for I felt that the future would require that I be better equipped. However, I was engaged in Christian ministry throughout the year. The days were very full and I was busy, handing in my assignments and projects just in time so that I could write the exams at the end of the year. In all the years that I was engaged in studying for exams, I never studied on Sundays. I do not judge others who do, but I felt that for me the day belonged to the Lord and I would always keep it altogether for him. It meant rising very, very early at times but I kept to this principle not to use the day which God had given to worship him, for my own use.

Suddenly it was September and I was to write examinations in November. I looked at all the books that I would have to master before the exams and my heart failed me. 'The only way I can get through, Mary, is for you to summarize this major theological work of 600 pages while I study the others, and then I will study your summaries!' Did ever any man ask his wife to do such an impossible thing? So we sat at the table, I at one end and Mary at the other, from early morning till late at night, week after gruelling week. I did not personally open the works of that theologian that year, but I studied Mary's summaries, wrote the exams and got a distinction in theology! It was Mary who should have got the distinction and the degree!

The week before Colin was born, I was asked to go to the Bible College in Cape Town as vice-principal under the principal, Mr Pienaar. I knew that it would come at one time or another. When I was a student at the old college in Kenilworth, one day I was reading the newspaper in the foyer of the main building. I closed the paper and turned around to go out, and at that moment, I had a sense of God saying to me, 'You're coming back here!' I stood rooted to the spot. I knew that it would happen.

In fact when we were at the Glenvar convention in Cape Town just after we were engaged, I drove Mary up to a view point on the top of a nearby mountain one night after the meeting. We were due to go to Johannesburg—that is 1,000 miles away—to do youth work. I looked over the valley below, covered in thousands of lights. In the midst of it all was the college. I said, 'Mary, your future is there.' There was no thought whatever in the minds of the Council that we were to go to the college, but God had spoken this into my heart, and I knew.

We journeyed the 1,000 miles from Johannesburg to Cape Town via the Transkei in our Volkswagen Beetle with a trailer loaded with goods and set up home in the flat over the entrance of the college. A new chapter had begun.

FAMILY LIFE

One night our little baby son, sleeping in the small adjoining room, was crying, so I rose, taking what I thought to be the milk bottle. I leant over him in his cot and tried to feed him. The more I tried to push the bottle into his mouth, the more he screamed. Mary came to my side and said, 'What are you doing?'

'I am trying to feed him,' I replied.

'But I have the bottle,' she said 'What do you have?' I looked, and saw, to my embarrassment, that I was trying to feed him with a tin of Johnson's baby powder. No wonder the baby screamed!

When he was only about two months old we were at a barbeque. Mary's back was turned and she did not see what I was doing. I took a chunk of meat, held it in my hand under the baby's mouth, then said loudly, 'Eat it, don't spit it out—chew it, boy!' Mary turned round and nearly had a fit! So we had fun!

On the 4th August, 1971, Heather Ann was born, so for eight days they were the same age. And then on 29th April, 1974, Christine Mary arrived. Mary had always had a strong conviction from the Lord that she would have three children, and so it turned out to be.

One Christmas we were to have an invasion of twenty-five relatives and friends for a week. Some would stay in the college but would all eat with us. Our small stove was far too small and we desperately needed a new cooker before they arrived. A grand sale of kitchenware was to take place in the northern suburbs so I hitched up the trailer and we clattered ten miles across the city to purchase a cooker. There were acres of goods and we found just the right cooker at the right price, but neither of us felt that we should buy it. We had the money but we felt that God was strangely restraining us and that we should leave it and go home. Puzzled, we left the very thing for which we had come. A few days later at the supermarket Mary saw a notice on their board, 'Stove for sale.' The phone number was given. As soon as she arrived home Mary phoned the number and found the owner to be a Christian friend. She was only too glad for us to come and pick it up—only too glad to give it to those in the work of God. We went immediately to her house and collected the cooker which was exactly the same model as the one we had seen in the sale and for which we now paid nothing! God again provided in an unusual and wonderful way. I am so glad we obeyed his leading!

**Mary and Colin as Colin graduates
with his doctorate**

Glenvar and Britain

The old college in Kenilworth where I had been trained had been sold and we had just moved to the six-acre plot in Constantia where the new college was to be built. Both are suburbs of Cape Town. The essential buildings were erected but there was a great deal of work still to be done on the grounds, and I was destined to be involved in this work. One moment I was in my overalls, then quickly into my suit for a lecture, and back again into my overalls! Grounds were laid out, trees were planted, a large retaining wall was built, areas were tarred and the grounds were generally beautified and made serviceable. It was a busy time.

A Christian friend from Postmasburg, Northern Cape, was there one day and he remarked that we needed a wall at the front of the college. I agreed. 'I'll send you some stone,' he said. He had jasper on his farm so he sent us twenty-five tons of jasper dug out of his farm for us to build a wall. This beautiful red jasper is a semi-precious material! So today the college stands behind a jasper wall. I don't suppose that there is another wall like it in all the world! A few American preachers visited the college a little later. They took photos of the wall and said, 'You can have the college; just give us the wall!'

I instituted the 'Soulwinner's Bible Memory System' in both English and Afrikaans, and this became an established and highly valued part of the course. I began a choir with all the students as members of the choir—unless they were tone deaf! Every year I would have to train the new ones, most of whom had never sung in a choir in their lives. Some job! Over the years we made two records which were later also recorded as cassettes. The choir was an excellent way to do deputation work, as ministers would invite the choir to sing and me to preach. So the college was increasingly known because of the choirs' activities in various places.

Chapter 15

We went on a tour across South Africa with the whole choir, visiting major centres and having the meetings organized by the district superintendents. The first tour, which was countrywide, was in six Volkswagen Kombis or minibuses and one or two cars. The first day we journeyed with about forty students all the way to Barkley West, near Kimberley, about 800 miles (1,300 kilometres) from Cape Town, sleeping that night at a camp site on the Vaal River. Early next morning I went for a walk along the river and God gave me a word to bring to the students. We gathered for prayer at 8.00am and I spoke for about twenty minutes. The presence of God was overwhelming and students began to seek God with all their hearts. There was great brokenness in the meeting. I remember one student going on his knees to another, making things right between them. My wife was a little late for the meeting and was amazed at this wonderful, sudden divine intervention. After all, these students were on the stretch for God. Now God had spoken again and they responded with all their hearts. That prayer meeting set the tone for the whole tour and we returned to the college, rejoicing in all that the Lord had done for us in the many large, packed meetings which were so full of the power and glory of the Lord. The choir sang in the Spirit, the touch of God was upon them and God greatly used them across the country.

Always the emphasis of the course was that the students should meet God in a radical way; that they should trust him for cleansing and for the fullness of the Holy Spirit; that they should know that there was much more land to be possessed and that they should strive for conformity to Christ. Their own walk with God was of paramount importance. If they were to be used by God they would have to know him and would have to live in his presence day by day! To that end there were the individual daily quiet times, and the corporate weekly time of devotion on the whole of every Friday morning. Those Friday mornings were sometimes so precious. So often God pervaded the college and we were conscious of his mighty melting and transforming power. Every term we had a half-night of prayer and God would sometimes invade these meetings transforming an ordinary prayer meeting to something quite extraordinary. Lives would be changed in his presence.

In 1972 we had an amazing visitation of God at the college. Students were so conscious of God's presence. The lectures continued but in the afternoons, when they were supposed to be studying, they put their studies aside and prayed, and prayed and prayed! The prayers were so Spirit-filled and powerful and from hearts that were obviously in touch with God. The corridors rang with song. Week after week this continued as they, and we all, basked in the presence of God. Eventually the term ended and the students returned to their homes. On their return the next term things were back to normal again. But what a term it was! We can only thank God for this touch of heaven on the college. When you have experienced that, you know what you want and are spoiled for everything else.

FURLOUGH IN BRITAIN

We had a furlough and we were allowed by the mission to take six months in Britain. God gave us a wonderful word before we left: 'Thou hast given me the heritage of those that fear thy name' (Psalm 61:5), and so it turned out to be, for the saints rallied to us and we were blessed in their fellowship and company. It was before the age of mass aeroplane transport, so Mary and I, with our two children at the time, embarked on a Union Castle ship bound for Britain. They sat comfortably in slings on our backs. The journey took eleven days and soon we were in the thick of meetings in UK. An Irish friend obtained a car for us and we journeyed all over England, Northern Ireland and Scotland. Our average was a meeting a day throughout the tour. It was a great time of rich blessing, but were we mad to go with two babies!

Mary had come to the Lord under the ministry of Rev. Duncan Campbell, in the Isle of Lewis, and later she, together with others in the team, had worked very closely with him. She and he were united in spirit with one aim and purpose—that of a God-glorifying revival. We had hoped to meet him, but he flew off to Switzerland for meetings a few days before we arrived. We were at her sister's home in Glasgow soon after we arrived, when she began to weep. 'What's the matter?' I asked.

'I don't know,' she replied.

'Have I done anything wrong?' I asked.

'No,' she said.

'Then why are you crying?' I asked.

'I don't know,' she answered. She wept all day. The next day we were told that Duncan had passed away the day before—the day she cried! It was an amazing communication of spirit to spirit over the many miles.

Chapter 15

Back in South Africa, the college course developed. I brought about changes to the curriculum and the library was increasingly used for assignments and projects. Local ministers gave lectures and my own sphere of lecturing increased. Even then, I wondered whether I was in the right place and whether I could be more effectively used elsewhere. Evangelist Ken Terhoven spoke at the college. An experienced man, he had a great work among the youth of South Africa and I wondered whether I should leave the college and join him. We talked together for an hour, and that night I laid this all before the Lord. In the morning my daily reading said, 'Arise ye, and depart; for this is not your rest: because it is polluted, it shall destroy you, even with a sore destruction' (Micah 2:10). It was a word from the Lord to my heart and I immediately wrote to Ken saying that I was no longer interested. I felt that the Lord had me in the right place at that time. Only a few months later, Ken left the work in which he was engaged and entered the ministry of the Church of England in South Africa. Had I not given heed to what God told me, and had I joined him, I would have been left high and dry with an impossible task ahead. God saved me from a serious blunder! Later I was asked to take the role of principal when Mr. Pienaar retired.

One morning the Lord spoke a word to my heart: 'He stayeth his rough wind in the day of the east wind' (Isaiah 27:8). It gripped me and was with me all morning. Suddenly I got a pain in my kidney. I had had a few kidney stones before and immediately recognized the intense pain. The doctor sent me to the hospital, where I writhed in agony as spasm upon spasm gripped me. This continued for some time and X-rays were taken periodically. Eventually the consultant came in and examined the last X-ray. He said, 'We'll prepare for surgery.' In those days that operation was a major event. 'No, let's have a final X-ray,' he said. They turned me over and took yet another X-ray. He returned some time later, looked at the X-ray, and exclaimed, 'Look, the stone is through! No need to operate!' I was saved—just one X-ray from the knife! I gratefully returned home. The Lord stayed his rough wind in the day of the east wind! The east wind is that burning, dry sirocco which comes to Israel straight from the desert, but even in that unpleasant east-wind experience, he did not allow it to become too rough and unbearable. The operation was cancelled and normality was restored. He stayed his rough wind! How precious is his Word to his trusting servants!

We took meetings all over in the Cape area and in the holidays were booked up at various conventions all over the country. Long journeys with the children in our Volkswagen Kombi were the order of the day. Wonderful memories!

Saturdays were always family days, and we saw to it that we were out with the children somewhere desirable. Often we were at Fish Hoek. The beach there and the walk along the rocky edge of the bay is always so relaxing. A favourite haunt was Boulders Beach, now the preserve of a penguin colony, but then a safe, private and very pleasant place for us all. Hout Bay, with its cold waters and beautiful sands, was another favourite spot. We had such fun and were able to unwind in the beautiful surroundings of what Sir Francis Drake called 'the fairest Cape in all the circumference of the earth'.

The AEB has convention centres in different places, one of which is in central Namibia. We drove there to speak at the meetings. After the convention we drove to the Etosha Game Reserve in the very north of the country with the children. We travelled from camp to camp enjoying seeing the animals in the wild. One day we stopped next to two lions lying with distended stomachs in the shade of a tree, and watched as a herd of wildebeest and zebras passed by. They saw that the lions had eaten well and would not move, so they walked fearlessly past, some even stepping between the extended legs of the lions. A jackal arrived on the scene and was dismayed to see his breakfast walking away. Surely if the lions rose and made a kill he would feed on the leavings—but the lions slept! He ran to one of the lions, grabbed its tail in his mouth and pulled. The lion lifted its head and roared. The jackal fled. But his hunger drove him back and once again he pulled the lion's tail. Again there was a roar and this time the jackal thought better of it and disappeared. It was a unique and marvellous cameo of wildlife—and we saw it!

SMOTHERED WITH KISSES

One meeting in Cape Town is worth mentioning. A church in a Coloured area of the Cape had special Fathers' Day meetings each year at which they asked a woman to speak and Mary was chosen that year so I drove her into this Coloured area for companionship and protection when there. She gave her message and then the pastor took over. He asked all the fathers to come up to the platform. I stood with the twenty-five to thirty fathers, and he said, 'Now we will allow you to congratulate the fathers.' They came, the vast army of women! I looked at him and said, 'We're for it?'

'Yes,' he said. 'We're for it!'

They came, the big fat ones, the well-dressed ones, the thin ones, the ancient ones, the toothless ones, the young pretty ones—they all swarmed on to the platform to give each father a congratulatory kiss with laughter and great merriment! I tried to turn my head so that the kiss would land on my cheek, but not a bit of it! It was mouth to mouth—the real thing! Never had I had such a dose of kissing! Mary was counselling a woman near the front. Oh how very diligent she was in that lengthy counselling session! *She* was not going up to congratulate all those fathers! Oh no, she was very busy with important spiritual work! Every now and again she would look up at me and try her utmost to contain herself, for she was bursting with laughter. On the way home I used my handkerchief to swab out my mouth for I did not know what colds, 'flu' or anything else I could have picked up—and Mary laughed! The moment we arrived at the house, I went for the Dettol bottle and gargled away to disinfect my mouth and throat. The cure was more deadly than the kisses. Thankfully I survived that memorable morning!

ONGOING STUDIES

My studies continued. I graduated from both UNISA and the Baptist Theological Seminary. I applied to the Baptist ministry and was interviewed by the grim-looking executive. I survived the ordeal, was accepted, ordained at a ceremony in Cape Town and placed on the ministerial list. I continued studying, doing a B.Th. Honours course with UNISA. Later in the UK, I continued with an M.Th. in conjunction with New College, Edinburgh, and later still, with a D.Th. from Trinity, USA.

When studying for Greek 2 to be able to enter into the M.Th. course, we had 142 pages of the Early Church Fathers to read in Greek. The examiner could ask us to translate any part of these passages, as well as, of course, passages from the New Testament. I was reading with some difficulty Diognetus in Greek, when suddenly I was gripped by the first verse of the ninth chapter. It was a fairly lengthy section, and God whispered into my heart that this was to be one of the questions. I met with another man who was writing the same subject to discuss the possibilities of the exam. I said to him, 'You can take it if you wish, but I feel that the Lord has told me that we are going to get Diognetus 9:1.' I prepared for the exam as best I could, and even as I walked towards the examination hall, I read Diognetus 9:1. I read it as I sat down waiting, and eventually had to put it aside as the examination papers were distributed. I opened the paper to find—yes, there it was: 'Translate Diognetus 9:1!' I did so with relish, God having instructed me to study it. Amazing! On other occasions in other exams, I had sometimes studied a section of the work just prior to the exam and was relieved to find that what I had just revised was the question I encountered in the exam. For that wonderful help I was so grateful, but this was quite different. Long before the exam, God guided me to the passage which I should learn for the exam. I just praised the Lord for his great kindness and guidance helping me to pass very comfortably.

About four years after our first adventure in the UK, we went again to Britain on a six-month furlough. Again our friend got a car for us and we drove all over the land, and again we had an average of a meeting a day for the whole period—but this time it was with three babies! Amazingly we coped and were able, as at the first, to spend some time with Mary's mother in Lewis. Many of these meetings were full of the presence of the Lord and we, together with the people, were thoroughly blessed. In the midst of this six-month tour of the UK, I flew to America for a six-week tour of meetings, while Mary took the children to the Isle of Tiree and spoke at several meetings across the island, before she went home to Lewis to wait for me. America was a blessed experience but it was just a taste of better things to come in later years.

At one place in Northern Ireland, a farmer lent us a small bungalow on his farm and arranged for babysitters to come to us every night for three weeks while we were out at meetings each night all over that area. We were travelling in the midst of the troubles in Northern Ireland and one night, coming back from a meeting, we passed through the city of Armagh. It was almost a battlefield of ramps, cement-filled drums, diversions, high wire to protect buildings and other ways to try to outwit the Irish Republican Army. In the middle of this saddened city, at about midnight, we were lost. If we went down one road or another, we might meet the IRA and we could die, so we stopped the car in a square and just sat still. A few moments later two policemen appeared. When they saw us, their right hands went to their chests to hold their revolvers and to prepare for the worst. They separated and walked cautiously towards us. We called out several times, 'We are lost!' and at last they believed us. With a great deal of careful manoeuvring, they approached and with great relief gave us safe directions home.

I well remember when the car came off the ferry from the mainland of Scotland to the Isle of Lewis to see Mary's family before we returned to South Africa, the Lord spoke a word to my heart, 'Mission accomplished!' It was great. God had gone before us and had helped us all the way. We had seen his hand at work and we rejoiced in his wonderful help and blessing.

Most of the members of the Faith Mission council

🔊 Emigration

I was involved in several councils of different missionary societies, was the secretary of the Cape Town Evangelical Council, and was thoroughly immersed in the work of God in the Cape, yet I somehow felt unsettled. How would God get me out of all these activities if we were to leave? And what of the college?

I walked up from the college one day to our house on the campus, and turned to look at the buildings. As I stood there, God spoke to me, and I knew that my ministry there was over. At that time I received a letter from Mrs Govan Stewart, the daughter of the founder of the Faith Mission in Scotland. It was a friendly letter but she asked that if I ever thought of leaving the AEB, I would give the Faith Mission first choice. She was not speaking from an official viewpoint at all, but that letter uprooted me! Just after that, their principal resigned and the post became vacant. In my heart I was away. Yet the Faith Mission appointed one of their own men, David Howden, to take the post. I had, as it were, to replant myself in the work from which I felt God was removing me, and for two years I continued in a strange world of knowing that I did not belong to that to which I was fully committed. There was a strange detachment from the immediate environment, although I was giving myself as much as ever to the work.

Two years after his appointment, tragically, David Howden walked into his house after washing his car, and dropped dead on the doorstep. Months passed and I heard nothing from the Faith Mission.

MOVING ON

I was taking part in a large campaign in Kimberley. The morning after the campaign, God spoke to me very strongly in my quiet time from John 21:6, 'Cast the net on the right side of the ship, and ye shall find. They cast therefore, and now they were not able to draw it for the multitude of fishes.' I could not get away from it. All the 800 miles (1,300 kilometres) on the road back to Cape Town, I pondered this text which had so strongly gripped my heart. God changed the place of their fishing, yet the method was the same. It was the same boat, yet they fished in a different place. What did it mean? On my arrival home, Mary presented me with a letter which had come just that day from Mr Dale, the General Director of the Faith Mission in Edinburgh, Scotland. 'Would I be interested in coming for an interview in the UK for a position in the Faith Mission?'

'Mary,' I said, 'it's the same boat only in a different place! God has already spoken to me through the passage I read this morning. This is of God.'

I flew to the UK for the interviews and had to stay overnight in Madrid. I was taken to an hotel and there, on the sixteenth floor, I went into my bedroom and fell on my knees. I opened the Bible at the place of my daily reading, and read, 'Get thee out of thy country, and from thy kindred, and come into the land which I shall show thee' (Acts 7:3). I knew that we would be going to Edinburgh, but I couldn't say that to those who were going to interview me! Eventually the call came and we were uprooted from beautiful Constantia, and taken over the sea to Britain. As we left, God whispered into my heart, 'This is the end of an era.' My great-grandfather had gone from Britain to South Africa with a Scottish wife, and now I was returning, at the age of forty-six, in July 1982, 121 years later, also with a Scottish wife and three children!

We flew from Johannesburg to Heathrow and then journeyed to Leicester to pick up the car which we had been given. We drove to Lewis to see Mary's family, later returning to Edinburgh. It was summer and everyone was out on campaigns. Mr Dale welcomed us to the principal's home and we settled in. Eventually the term began and I was cast into the role of lecturer and administrator once again.

The girls were happy in their nearby primary school, but Colin was very uncertain in the large high school with 1,800 pupils. He did well, coming first in a number of subjects, so well, in fact that I went to see the headmaster. 'The others don't want to learn,' stated the headmaster.

'If he is so bright,' I said, 'why not put him up a year?'

'They don't want to learn either,' admitted the head.

We knew then that we would have to move him from that comprehensive school. Where would we go? Mary lifted the phone and called George Heriot's High School—a private school. He passed the entrance exam and was offered a place. It would cost £461 per term and there were three terms. How could we ever afford this? We stood in the bedroom and held each other as we prayed. It was a moment of destiny. Could we? Would we trust God to provide for our son? After two years we would be able to apply for state aid, but for two years we would have to pay ourselves. Yes! Yes! We would trust God. No-one knew of our situation but a week before the term began, the bank informed us that someone had deposited £500 into our account! We don't know who it was, but that was the first term paid. Later Mary was asked to speak at a meeting in Lewis, so, it being the school holidays, she took the children for ten days to the Hebrides. She paid for petrol, for gifts, for goodies for the children, for toiletries and other things without taking note of what she was spending.

On their return, Mary gave me her bag with the words, 'Look after that, there's quite a bit of money in it.' I did not expect much from a brief Scottish tour, so I left it for quite some time. Perhaps there would be thirty or forty pounds, I thought. Eventually I took it up and began to count—100, 200, 300, 400, then £461 exactly! I nearly went through the roof! The exact amount that was needed! One man had given her a roll of bank notes consisting of £300. (Although we have been in his home many times since, he has never given us a penny since that day, but when it was so badly needed, God prompted him to open his hand.) I shouted in amazement, and then said, 'Oh, but the tithe.'

She said, 'There's another little zip pocket in the bag with some change in it.' I looked, and there was £46! The £46 was placed in our 'tithes and offerings' envelope, and the £461 banked. Our son went to school the next day with a cheque for £461!

I was asked to become the editor of the Faith Mission magazine called *Life Indeed*. I refused at first as I needed to settle in to the college work, but a year later took on the editorial duties and this I did for about sixteen years, writing many articles over this period of time.

A SEEKER IS SAVED

One day I was standing in the foyer of the college, when a young lady knocked at the door. I invited her in and asked what we could do for her.

Chapter 16

'I've come to get to know the Faith Mission,' she replied.

'Do you want to come for training?' I asked.

'I don't know,' she said. 'You see, I was in the main street in Fort William when a lady spoke to me about my soul. She had to go, so she said, "What you need, my girl, is the Faith Mission, and here's their address." So I've come all the way from Glasgow to see about the Faith Mission.'

'Do you know the Lord? Are you saved?' I asked.

'Saved from what?' she enquired.

She was so ripe! It was just such a joy to lead her to the Lord and to rejoice with her in her new-found salvation. What an amazing event! She made the journey all the way from Glasgow, a distance of about forty miles (seventy kilometres), on her own. She looked for and found the college and had the courage to knock on the door with no reason for doing so. The fish swam a long way to put itself on the hook!

She found a Bible-believing church, became a bright Christian and married a fine young Christian man. They emigrated to Australia and have established a Christian family there.

**The Faith Mission College in
Edinburgh**

Moving the college

I had been involved in one great college move in Cape Town and now here I was in another. The old college in Ravelston, Edinburgh, had a very limited collection of books as a library. It was just not sufficient for modern-day teaching. We needed a library. I drew up plans for changes to be made in the existing buildings but we all realized that that would not be sufficient.

The college executive met for four days of prayer and planning at the end of 1983 for the centenary of the Mission which was to take place in 1986. I presented to the executive, in a ten-page document, a series of changes to the work pattern and a plea for the college to move to new premises. After some discussion, the executive took the momentous decision to buy or build a new College and convention centre. Willie Porter, the leader of the work in Ireland, leaned back in his chair and said, 'This is the biggest decision the Faith Mission council has ever taken in all its history!' If I had not come from outside the mission, viewing the whole picture objectively, I doubt whether any change would have been made, for everyone was strongly attached to the old college where they had been so greatly blessed. Had the principal been happy with the old college, they would simply have continued there. I think that of all the things I was enabled by God's grace to do in the Faith Mission, this proposition was probably the most important of all.

GILMERTON FACILITY

The search was on and after viewing several sites, we eventually discovered buildings in Gilmerton, Edinburgh, which had been a school for troublesome girls. We eventually purchased the school. In fact two hours before the graduation on Friday 27th June, 1986, the solicitors informed the Mission that our bid was successful. The director made the great announcement at the meeting and the choir rose to sing 'Glory, glory, hallelujah, Our God is marching on!' A great step of faith had been taken! The old college and other properties were sold; gifts came in and we moved in, debt-free. It was a huge undertaking. Those were exciting days and we were all involved. Many areas had to be gutted, replanned and rebuilt before the students arrived. It was a case of demolition, construction and decoration. People with various skills, and with no skills at all, came from every part of the British Isles to help build the house of the Lord. It was a race against time but it was done and on the 8th January, 1987, the first meal was served in the new dining hall from the new kitchen, and the new term began in the new College! Tremendous! Hallelujah! The Annual Faith Mission Edinburgh Convention now takes place at the College which has space to house the workers and others who book in for the week's meetings.

The library was at that time merely a collection of 4,000 books to which little reference was made. God sent us a librarian who is also a theologian, and Norma Downie and I worked together on that library. We discarded numbers of books which were not of use, and then began the great work of building the library. Librarians came and helped classify the books until today there are 15,000 volumes, all classified. It is a very worthwhile collection with little or no padding, and it forms the basis for the teaching at the College. Norma made an enormous contribution to the College programme, building up the library in a wonderful way. The better the library, the better the assignments; the better the assignments, the better the understanding, grasp, and hopefully, presentation of scriptural truth.

We were still living on the northern side of the city, and I had to drive across each day to the southern side. We needed a house for the principal somewhere near to the new college. We looked at several and we placed our bids, but failed each time. The Scottish system is that your lawyer bids for you and you don't know what anyone else has bid. Our bidding was always too low! One day I walked into a house and I was conscious that the Lord was confirming that this was the house he had for us. In my heart I knew that this was the one. The price was quoted as: 'Offers above £121,000.' Three of us met, and in the director's office we decided that we would bid on this house. That night I went through all the figures before the Lord. I waited upon him on each thousand above the £121,000 required. When I reached £131,000 I sensed that the Lord was confirming this to me, so we put in our bid at £131,667. The next day we were informed by the lawyer that we had been gazumped—that is, someone had bid way above our amount. I was astounded. I knew that this was not of God and said so. 'The devil has stolen this house from us,' I said. 'God gave me the price and gave me this house, and the devil has taken it from me.' The director smiled wryly and walked away. I said under my breath, 'You can laugh, my boy, but I know what I know!'

Even my wife asked, 'If God gave you the figure, why did God not give you the house?'

I looked at her and said reproachfully, 'Job also had a wife!' Job's wife, as you know, opposed him in his troubles. We have laughed many times about her being 'Job's wife'!

Two months passed, when suddenly the director was informed that the property was again on the market. The buyer could not raise the money and it was again up for sale. We met hastily and agreed to bid the same amount. It was placed that same day, and the next day we were informed by the lawyer that our offer had been successful and that the property was ours! The relief and joy, not only that we at last had a house, but that I had heard the voice of God and had found him faithful to execute that which he had spoken to me in my innermost being!

I enrolled all the students in the choir which I conducted, and we went to numerous churches in Edinburgh and its environs singing, with me preaching, making the college known. For the centenary of the Mission in 1986, this choir was central to the procedures as we went on a mighty centenary tour in a well-worn coach which had been donated to the college, throughout the counties of England, Scotland and Ireland. We journeyed from the Isle of Lewis in the north of Scotland, to Launceston, Cornwall, in the south of England, and to Ipswich in East Anglia. We were all over Northern Ireland and also to meetings in the South as well. It was a wonderful time of blessing and bonding. Some of those prayer meetings were memorable indeed and filled with the presence of the Lord. One particularly in the Launceston Methodist Church broke all our hearts. A student named Aileen prayed and was mightily helped. We wept for fifteen minutes in the presence of the Lord as she led us in mighty intercession. When she said 'Amen' I wondered who would dare touch this meeting now. A young girl called Alison took it up and began to pray. God was with her in great power, and again we wept as Alison led us into God's presence for another fifteen minutes. What wonderful moments! Rev. Tommy Shaw and I did most of the preaching but many others made great contributions to the spirit of the meetings. They really were great and blessed times! We made a cassette of the singing and this was distributed widely.

HEART ATTACK AND BYPASS OPERATION

Unfortunately, I had a heart attack in 1991 and was off for several months. However, I survived and continued with a very full programme.

In 1998, I was in America for a convention in Pennsylvania with the Amish people. There were about 1,500 young people and I spoke just once. That night I had a massive pain in my chest. I was taken to the hospital and given an angiogram. The doctors said, 'You need heart bypass surgery, and you need it now. Don't leave the hospital, and don't think of going home—that plane won't turn around for you!' I phoned my doctor in Edinburgh and the insurance agency sent out a cardiologist from London who examined me and said that he thought we could fly home. Mary and our daughter Heather flew out to be with me. We flew back and Mary says, 'I sat in the middle with the two doctors snoring away. One was supposed to be sick and the other supposed to be looking after him!'

'When will they do the operation?' I asked the London doctor.

'This week or the next,' was his reply.

But when the Edinburgh doctors examined me they said, 'You are number 641 on the list! Maybe you will be able to have an operation in more than a year's time!' With my programme I knew that I would be dead before that time. There were committee meetings, programmes, lecturing, preaching, administration, organization etc!

'How can it be done immediately?' I asked.

'Go private,' the doctor answered. 'It will cost about £10,000.'

So, if you have money you live, and if you don't have money you die!

I lay in the hospital wondering what should be done, when in walked someone whom I had seen at our church in Edinburgh. She had come in to visit her husband, whom I did not know, and who was in the same ward for two days, merely for tests. We stood at my bedside, Mary and I with this couple, and we talked for ten minutes. The next day she phoned Mary and said, 'When we were at Colin's bedside yesterday, I sensed the presence of God more than I have done for many, many years. We are wealthy and would like to help.' We hardly knew them but the husband, who does not attend that church, came to me in the ward and offered to pay for the operation. I remonstrated at once but he was insistent and gave the money for the operation to take place. Amazing that we were in the same ward together for just those two days! God knows how to organize things! I was transferred to Glasgow and the operation took place a few days later, undertaken by a South African doctor to whom I spoke in Afrikaans and said, 'When you handle my heart, just look carefully and you will see written there, "Preach the Word!"' As a matter of fact, four people kindly and generously offered to pay for the operation.

Mary had put out a letter in the meantime to our friends asking for prayer for me. And suddenly, without our asking for any money at all, it began to roll in from individuals, from fellowships and from churches, until, three months later, we had the amount needed and were able to repay the man who had given us the money in the first place to enable the operation to be done! Some well organized operation! What an omniscient God!

When we first came to Edinburgh I told Tillie Thompson, the able college secretary, that I would be leaving the college when I was sixty-two. She just laughed at such talk—but God had whispered this into my heart. The years passed. Dr Sandy Roger who was on the Faith Mission council was available two years before I was to retire, but would not be available when I was due to retire. I therefore suggested that we consider him as the next principal. I would then leave the college early and the next era at the college could begin. This eventually took place, and, as he had a house in Edinburgh, we were allowed to stay in the principal's house. The transition was made at the college graduation in June 1999, when I was sixty-two with one day to go!

'Didn't I tell you, Tillie?' I asked.

'Yes you did, several times, but I never thought that it could happen,' she replied. When we left, there were sixty students at the College. We were blessed to close on a high note and the Faith Mission council honoured me with the title of Principal Emeritus, a title never given before. We were still on the Faith Mission workers' list, for I had not yet retired, but were released to preach all over as God opened doors.

Lecturing to Faith Mission students

Ministry

W e spent seventeen years at the Faith Mission College in Edinburgh. We had a team of able, spiritual workers on the staff as well as other lecturers from churches in the city. I lectured on Biblical Doctrine, Romans, 1 John, Timothy, Homiletics, Church History, Soul-winning and anything else where a lecturer was needed to step into the gap! I began public lectures on Monday nights and these are still going strong. I also began the annual Duncan Campbell Memorial Lectures which have been a source of inspiration to many as lecturers have spoken of revival. My most treasured time with the students was the weekly Friday morning prayer meeting, which I often addressed and which was mainly a time of prayer. There were some wonderful mornings when the lives of the students were transformed in God's presence. In addition we had a half-night of prayer each term, and the devotional aspect of the college was uppermost in all our minds. Having a radical encounter with God, and being equipped by the cleansing power of the blood of Jesus and the fullness of the Spirit, is essential for those in the service of the King. This was held before the students all the time. To have the sacred anointing they needed to know his presence and to walk in the light in close fellowship with him.

Every now and again we were away to meetings here and there across the nation. One such series was the Keswick event in Wales where I gave the Bible Readings. One night the Lord stepped into the meeting and there was such a heavenly silence that it could be felt. There was such an intense sense of God that we were hushed. My words fell with solemn weight in a silence that was awesome. After I said, 'Amen', no-one moved. One felt that one could almost not breathe lest one disturb the presence of the Lord. It lasted for thirty minutes, then one or two brave people prayed briefly. Our souls were bowed to the earth and we walked away from that meeting in amazement, with godly fear and awesome reverence, for we had met the King. Anything could have happened. The leader of the convention said later to me, 'This convention has never had such a meeting!'

I think of another occasion in the Isle of Harris when the power of God was such that I had to stop preaching as a Christian worker could not contain his tears in God's presence.

A few weeks later in that same church Mary gave her testimony with such power and beauty that we just sat there weeping. She returned to her seat next to me, and that same divine silence settled on the meeting. No-one moved. At last, after about fifteen minutes, Mary turned her head and whispered to the man sitting behind her, to whom we were going for tea after the meeting, 'You had better put the kettle on.'

He whispered back, 'I'll not be the first to move in this meeting!' And we sat on.

Eventually the minister rose at the back and walked slowly down the aisle lifting a few song books. He placed them on the table at the front, looked around, and said softly in the silence, 'Oh, I'd better sit down,' and moved back to his seat. Gradually the people began to move. I went to the door to greet them as they left. There were no happy-go-lucky, smiling, friendly greetings that night. Oh no! They hardly spoke. Just a nod of the head and a strong squeeze of the hand as they slipped away into their cars, bearing the presence of God with them. Oh, how utterly wonderful is the presence of God! When you have tasted that you are spoiled for everything else. They can come with their bands, their choirs, their well-ordered meetings but you have heard a Voice, and that Voice you long to hear again; you have sensed a Presence and that Presence you long to sense again!

GOD BREAKS THROUGH

I was speaking at the Keswick event in Bradford, England, one year. We were having good times but I longed for God to break through into the meetings. The elderly couple with whom I was staying expressed a strong desire to take me into the Yorkshire Dales on the Saturday afternoon. They had been so kind to me during the week that I did not want to disappoint them by refusing their kind offer. I would love to see the Yorkshire Dales, but not right at that point. I was in a fight; I was in the heat of the battle! I needed to see God invade the scene and I had only one meeting left.

That they did not understand, so into the Yorkshire Dales we sallied. I prayed, 'Lord please take care of me and give me a broken heart.' I knew that my heart would need to be broken if I would see the victory of the Lord in the meeting. 'Isn't that lovely,' she would say, as she admired some beautiful scene.

'Oh yes,' I answered.

'And look at that,' she said again and again, to which I answered in appreciative monosyllables. The truth was that God was answering my prayer. My heart was simply broken. I saw the beauties of nature but they did not hold me. I was in my own world with a breaking heart sitting alone in the back of the car. We came to the end of the journey up in the hills, and got out to enjoy tea and cream scones. I excused myself and walked around the building until I had found a corner where no-one could see me. I leant into the corner and wept. I simply broke my heart for the people and for the meeting, but most of all that God would come and pour his Spirit into that final meeting. I call it my agony time. It happened. Eventually I washed my face and enjoyed their company at the tea table. On the way back home it was all repeated and I responded appropriately, but I knew that I had touched the throne. That night we had a great victory and God broke through in great power and many Christians sought God to cleanse them as they consecrated themselves again to God. It was worth the tears, worth the broken heart, worth the soul-anguish. That is the price that needs to be paid if one is to see the Lord work in power and glory. And because it is so costly, not many are prepared to pay that price, with the result that they simply have ordinary ministries. May the Lord save us from ministries which are weak and ineffective, but give us meetings which are permeated with the wonder, beauty and power of his glorious presence—but that only comes with soul travail!

The Christian unions of all the Scottish universities had a day of prayer and fasting. The student officials wore special tee-shirts and students assembled from all over the country at the Caird Hall in Dundee. It was a great privilege for Mary to be asked to speak to the assembled students. There were about 500 in the hall. The Bible was simply read by one student after another for long periods; some songs were sung led by a small instrumental group, prayers were offered and then Mary spoke. She took as her text Isaiah 59:1, 2, 'Behold, the LORD's hand is not shortened, that it cannot save; neither his ear heavy, that it cannot hear: but your iniquities have separated between you and your God, and your sins have hid his face from you, that he will not hear.' God was with her in great power and the Spirit of the Lord settled on the whole hall. When she finished there was opportunity given for prayer and there were many tears as students sought God afresh for his cleansing and empowering. It was a great day of blessing in the presence of the Lord.

We have had the privilege of speaking at meetings all over Britain and Northern and Southern Ireland. It has been wonderful to have been able to enter into the labours of so many of God's choice servants, and to sense, on so many occasions that melting presence of the Almighty. How good is our God!

SERVING TOGETHER

It has been wonderful for Mary and me to have been able to work together over the years. On one occasion at the Killedeas Camp Convention in Co. Fermanagh, Northern Ireland, there were several hundred people present on the Sunday afternoon. As she was speaking, she said in Afrikaans, 'Maak reg, ek is siek.' It was said in the flow of the sentence and no-one (apart from me) knew what she had. She said: 'Get ready, I am sick.' I left my seat in the congregation and stepped up on to the platform taking my seat immediately behind her. At an appropriate moment she said, 'I am not feeling well and my husband will continue.' With that she stepped off the platform and disappeared, leaving me to complete her ministry! I stepped into the gap and continued where she had left off. The spirit of the meeting was in no way affected and we all rejoiced in the way in which the Lord undertook as I continued along the lines that my wife had begun!

On another occasion I suddenly felt ill as I stepped up to read the Scriptures in a packed church. I saw that I would not be able to do it and I handed the reading to a colleague while I staggered back to my seat. I knew that I could not continue, so as the reading was drawing to a close, I looked over to Mary and said, 'You take over.' She rose as if it were all arranged, and poured out her heart to the great blessing of all who were present, while I was taken off to bed!

INTERNATIONAL MINISTRY

Not only were we privileged to speak in the UK, but abroad as well. On several occasions we have been back to South Africa to speak at the main convention of the AEB as well as to that of the Bethel work and some other meetings as well. Doors opened and we were in Korea, Japan, India, Canada, America, Israel, Holland, France, Switzerland, Germany, and Belgium. In Canada we spoke at a number of church meetings as well as a series of meetings for the Faith Mission in Canada. We spoke at camps at both of their camp centres in the Toronto area and across in the Vancouver area. At a camp in Germany I spoke eleven times in one week, and often we were hushed in the presence of the Lord. Several times virtually the whole congregation responded in acts of dedication to God.

We were twice in Australia and on both occasions we spoke at a camp convention in the Adelaide hills. At the second convention there were some young people who took things very lightly and were only in the meetings because they had to be there. One night as I was speaking, the lights went out. We were plunged into blackness. The young folk sat at the back and passed notes to each other without much interest in what was being said, but the sudden darkness put a stop to that. Torches shone upon me and my notes and those young folk had to pay attention. At last God got through to them and they listened! The Lord came into that meeting and when I made an appeal, about twenty of them sought the Lord. It was a great victory.

We began to go to America a few years before we left the college and then for about ten years we went on preaching tours in America for six weeks at a time each year—sometimes twice a year. We normally averaged about a meeting a day throughout the times we were in the States. These were times of great blessing when God revealed himself to us and descended on many occasions where there was great brokenness in the people where we ministered. We were in many states and in different denominations, mainly Baptist. There are many different brands of Baptists in the States. Mary accompanied me throughout these tours and often gave her testimony and spoke at women's meetings—with remarkable effects! At one place her testimony to revival was taken up on DVD and this has subsequently been circulated widely.

In one state we were being driven by car half way to the next place of meetings, being met at a restaurant by the folk to whom we were going. On the way there I said to the man who was driving us there, 'Floyd, I just want to thank you so very much for being willing to take this day off and drive us across.'

'Oh no!' he said, 'You have got it all wrong. You see I'm part of the gospel team. The gospel must be preached, so the preacher must be taken to the different places where the gospel is to be preached. The people who take the preacher are simply part of the team. It's my great privilege to take the preacher so that the Kingdom of God can be extended. It's no sacrifice, brother, it's a joy and a privilege for me to be part of the ongoing work of the gospel!' What a great attitude he had!

One day at home I received an email from the leader of the Southern Baptists in Oklahoma State. He said that he had been sent a cassette of a message that I had preached and had listened to it seven times. All he had was my name on the cassette, but he ran this as a Google search and found our web site. Would I come and speak to their men? It was their Annual Convention on Evangelism to which we went, and it was to 5,000 pastors and delegates, in Oklahoma City. Mary spoke to the women and I had several opportunities to speak to the whole conference. Dr Henry Blackaby and I were the main speakers at the event. The last evening arrived and an Afro-American named Gary Strong preached first. It was a mighty utterance, eloquent and powerful. I was sitting with Mary in the front seat and I turned to her and simply said, 'What am I going to say now? How can I follow that?'

She looked at me and said with conviction: 'Just get up there and preach!' I did, and God was wonderfully with me. The atmosphere was charged with the power of God, and when I opened the altar for people to seek God, scores of pastors and others knelt at the front or bent low in prayer in great brokenness in different parts of that vast church. Some were even prostrate. I came down from the platform and stood at the front. Gary Strong was about twenty yards away, also at the front. Our eyes met and he came to me, quickly stepping over the praying figures. 'My brother!' he exclaimed, 'My brother, oh my brother!' With that he flung his arms around me, squeezed me almost breathless and lifted me off my feet in a great bear hug. I think he appreciated the message!

In Japan we spoke at the great JEB convention in Kobe. I gave the morning Bible readings and one morning God simply fell on that meeting. The leader made an appeal and more than a hundred folk sought God at the front of the hall. He prayed with them from the pulpit and sent them back to their seats for the final hymn when suddenly a great and bitter cry rent the air. A young pastor, half way down the hall, was bent over in an intense desire after God. Another pastor ran to him but he would not be comforted. Twice more he cried loudly to God. And then the whole congregation sought God in prayer! I came down from the platform and stood at the front. Suddenly there were about thirty pastors standing with me. They began to weep and we all sank to our knees. One senior pastor held my wrist with his head on my elbow which shook up and down as he simply wept. They prayed brokenly and eventually rose to their feet. We stood in awed silence and examined the carpet when one began to pray again, and again we were all on our knees with an awesome sense of God filling the place. These are the 'unemotional' Japanese!

We were driven to another convention on an island in Japan, crossing the longest suspension bridge in the world to get there, where missionary Hugh Brown from Northern Ireland translated for me. At the close of one of these meetings, so many folk sought God that the pastor said simply to Hugh, 'Tell him to come back. I don't know what to do with this meeting!' We closed with a moving time of prayer.

We were booked to go to Japan to speak at a convention for missionaries where about 400 missionaries would gather, and there were also to be three other Japanese conventions. The bookings were made two years before the events. Six months before we were to go, I became very uneasy about going to Japan. Phone calls and emails followed. I could give no reason for my unease. Eventually I said, 'Have you printed the leaflets yet?'

'No, but we are about to do so.'

'Then cancel our coming and get another speaker,' I said. It was incomprehensible to them and to me. Why was I throwing away this wonderful opportunity to minister to so many of God's servants as well as to the many Japanese at the conventions? However, it was cancelled and we filled in the now vacant space with other meetings. We were at a conference on revival in Bridgend, South Wales. Mary spoke one night in the large tent and the following morning we were in a meeting in the Bible College at which Rev. Vernon Higham was speaking and where the meetings were being held, when she suddenly collapsed. The meeting moved to an adjacent room and the ambulance was called. An experienced nurse was there and she said to me, as Mary lay breathing with guttural sounds as if she were breathing her last, 'Take her hand, she's dying right now.'

Chapter 18

She was transferred to the hospital and remained there for a week before we could get back home. The doctors had prescribed too many drugs and her heartbeat had been seriously reduced to the point where she very nearly slipped away. It was when she was in hospital that we should have left for the meetings in Japan. God knew all along and had stopped me finalizing the Japanese arrangements because we could not have gone with Mary so ill. It was all clear now! I am so glad that I heard his voice and obeyed. I could easily have brushed aside his leading and convinced myself that what I was feeling was utter nonsense, but thankfully I was sensitive enough to obey God. Paul was 'forbidden of the Holy Ghost to preach the word in Asia' (Acts 16:6). I too felt that same restraint and was grateful for his guidance.

We were ministering with others, at a 'Heart-Cry for Revival' conference held in the church where Dr Andrew Murray ministered in Wellington, South Africa. Mary and I were both to speak at a meeting in the afternoon. Mary testified and then it was my turn, but time was marching on and we were due to eat at 6.00pm. I was at the height of my message when I saw that the large clock before me indicated 5.50pm. I still had ten minutes. I preached on for another twenty or twenty-five minutes. The Spirit of God swept over the gathering, and I made an appeal. The clock still displayed 5.50pm! There was great power and liberty and many people surged forward to meet with God and to do business with him at the front of that great church. I looked at the clock and it still indicated 5.50 pm! It had stopped at the right moment and given me the liberty to draw the message to a satisfactory conclusion, which I could not have done had I felt rushed at the end of the meeting. God met with many people that day, and all because the clock stopped. God in his providence arranged it perfectly!

I have been invited to undertake preaching tours in various countries, such as Pakistan, Mongolia, Papua New Guinea, several African countries, Korea, Japan, Australia (again) and others. However, I did not feel that I could take on so much and declined with much regret.

I love writing and began in South Africa with a little work on soul-winning. This was translated into Afrikaans and later reprinted in both languages. I followed that with a little work for young people called *Youth Challenged* which was also translated into Afrikaans. I then gathered my poems in a small volume called *Scattered Pearls*. When at last I could do some serious work in the UK, I wrote *Heritage of revival*, the story of revivals in the work of the Faith Mission for the centenary of the Faith Mission. Other books followed, two of which, *The Authority of the Bible* and *How to resist Temptation*, have been translated into several languages. The former is now in Arabic and made available for Moslems! Never in my wildest dreams had I imagined that I would be ministering to Moslems, but it happened. I just praise the Lord for the privilege he has given me. God helped me to write a devotional commentary on the book of Joshua and a small doctrinal work called *Great Gospel Words*. One book was particularly used and published four times in two years. It is the story of the 1949 revival in the Hebrides, Scotland. This book, called *Sounds from Heaven*, has gone far and wide and has opened many doors for speaking and for numbers of interviews on radio programmes. And the writing goes on ...!

Mary has been singing the gospel in Gaelic for the BBC for the last fifty years. They have a series of her songs on CD and every few weeks she is on one or other of their programmes. (She was paid about £60 at the beginning when she recorded them and not a penny since!) Consequently she is a well known figure in the Highlands of Scotland and has been on several panels discussing various subjects in Gaelic. The BBC has recorded an hour-long documentary on her life which was shown on television in Gaelic but with English subtitles. She has been allowed to produce a CD of twelve of the songs which they have been playing all these years, and this has now been done. I have had quite a bit of ministry in the Hebrides and we have been asked on several occasions to fill vacant pastorates of the Church of Scotland on the islands. This we have done for a six-week or two-month period and this has been a useful and blessed experience as I have taken on the role of minister for those periods.

Broxburn residence

**Christine, Heather, Colin Jr.,
Colin and Mary**

God's provisions

Both the AEB and the Faith Mission are 'faith missions'. That means that the workers go out without mentioning their needs, and they trust the Lord to provide for them. Each pair of workers is responsible for their own needs, and they are expected to pray those needs in. But if not enough money comes in to meet their needs, the statements which they fill in monthly or quarterly, reflect their condition, and headquarters, if it has money, meets the deficit. There are no accumulated funds from which the workers are paid. Each section of the work must carry itself and all receive a small amount each month for their personal needs. In the Faith Mission all the workers are on the same level of pay, from the chief executive and the principal, to the youngest recruit—all receive the same small amount each month. The workers are allowed to receive personal gifts. Of course there is a small household allowance and a scaled children's allowance, but neither the AEB nor the Faith Mission will make anyone rich! Their riches are of a spiritual kind. The lives of the workers are those of intense self-denial and sacrifice—and God prompts people to stand with them in the work of the Kingdom. Christian people recognize the worth of what they do and stand with them in prayer and in practical support.

Many, many instances of divine intervention and provision could be cited. In so many instances, the tiny, almost insignificant provisions of God are some of the most precious, for we realize that he cares for us in the smallest detail. When we had need of money, it came, and when we had no need, no money came. God is an amazing bookkeeper.

LIVING BY FAITH

Let me tell of God's provision in the realm of cars. This is a wonderful testimony to his gracious kindness and love.

Chapter 19

Mary was released by the Faith Mission to respond to the many invitations coming her way from churches all over the country. Someone gave her a little Vespa scooter and with this she negotiated the traffic in the cities in England and rode all the way to her home in Lewis! This was upgraded to a Lambretta scooter some time later. A godly fisherman in Shetland gave her a brand new Volkswagen Beetle to pursue the work, and this was her 'home' for a number of years as she journeyed from one town to another in gospel ministry; it was later written off in an accident. With the insurance from the write-off she was able to get a Ford Cortina which served her well until she gave the car to the Faith Mission. The General Director would not hear of it and gave Mary £300 for the car. This she gave to those who reprinted her book, *I was saved in revival.*

At the beginning of the AEB youth work I was given a two-year-old red Volkswagen Beetle. Then the babies came and the family grew. Friends who had a medium-sized green and white Volkswagen station wagon called us one day and told us to collect the vehicle. We were needing two cars at that time as Mary had her programme of meetings and I had mine.

Eventually we gave the red Volkswagen Beetle to another worker in the mission and we were able to use the car which the Mission provided as well as the little station wagon. That eventually showed signs of age and we were needing something more substantial.

One day in Cape Town, we received a phone call from the man who had given us the Beetle to come and pick up a red Volkswagen Kombi (a small minibus). Someone else no longer required two large boxes specially built for a Kombi. When the middle seat was removed they fitted exactly into the gap from the back seat to the front seat. Their tops were covered with a three-inch layer of foam rubber. On the long journeys which we took for convention ministry in different parts of the country during the holidays, we spread a blanket over the whole back seat area forming a large double bed. It was a wonderful provision for the children. All our luggage was in the boxes and the children had space to endure long, hot journeys across the country.

Before we left South Africa in 1982, a dear ageing spinster friend of Mary's in the Leicester area told us that when we arrived in the UK, we should come to their home and take her Morris 1800, as she had no further use for it. The very day that we arrived in Britain, we were provided with the gift of a spacious car. The Mission provided me with a car but for Mary's meetings and the children's extramural activities, it was wonderful.

It later came to the end of its existence and had to be replaced. A retired missionary heard of our need and sent us £1,300 for another vehicle. We contacted a Christian motor firm in Northern Ireland and enquired as to a vehicle in that price range. He said, 'I have an Opel Kadet which cost me £1,600. It has just come in. I will give it to you for the amount that I paid for it.' A Faith Mission worker in Ireland heard about this and at his last meeting at a campaign told this story to the congregation asking them to give a love gift for the remaining money. It came to exactly £300! The £1,600 was there, provided by a missionary who had been living by faith in Africa and by a love gift from a Northern Ireland congregation.

This car eventually had to be replaced. Friends near Oxford gave us their Austin Montego. A young lady wanted to give her little Fiat Uno 'a good home' so she gave us the car before she embarked on her missionary venture. This enabled us to give the Austin to other friends in the city.

We were about to retire and there was no word of a car from any quarter. I could not understand this for the Lord had provided so many cars for us over the years; surely he would not leave us now. Why was heaven silent? The college car which I was driving, a Peugeot 405, was ageing. The General Director said one day to me, 'When you were absent from the council meetings in Northern Ireland, the council decided that you could take the car. I must have forgotten to tell you!' There was I wondering why the Lord was not providing, when he had provided all the time—only the Director had forgotten to tell me!

We drove this for some time when one day it just died with multiple injuries on the huge Newbridge roundabout near Edinburgh! We acquired another Mission car, also a Peugeot 405, for which we had to pay the repairs after a write-off, and this kept us going for a while.

One day a doctor friend offered us her Skoda. It was four years old and was in good shape. So we gave away to our son the one we had repaired, as he needed a car at that time, and then ran this little 1.3 litre Skoda Felicia.

It was a write-off in an accident when someone bumped into us from behind. The insurance company gave us £1,500 for the vehicle's remains! Our son was not using his car all that much so we were able to use that for the time being. What were we to do? Out of the blue came a phone call from a friend who is in the Lord's service and also living by faith. He said, 'We have had a windfall and I am sending you £5,000 for a new car.' That meant that we had £6,500 for a car. We have a contact in Northern Ireland who was able to get us a year-old Vauxhall Astra, at trade price, some £2,000 lower than the retail price; so by adding just a little to that which we had available for a car, we were able to purchase a safe and good quality vehicle. Amazing!

I guess that not many people can testify to the fact that they have been given thirteen cars for the work of the Lord. They were not new nor anywhere near it, (with the exception of the Astra), but they got us from A to B and served us wonderfully in his work. We praise the Lord for this wonderful provision.

MANNA IN THE MORNING

When our children were at university they nearly always brought their friends back home from church for Sunday dinner. There were often more than twelve around the table. At that precise time Europe was suffering from a very strange policy on food. There had been over-production and there was a 'meat mountain' and a 'butter mountain' of excess food which was being distributed all over. Loads had been sent to a school for handicapped children nearby and the authorities there asked us whether we would like some of this high-quality food. It came, not only to the college, but also to us. There were tins of mince and tins of stew, as well as 22 kilogram boxes of beautiful boneless meat. When these boxes arrived, I took them to the abattoir and had the box of meat cut into manageable sizes to store in our deep freeze. For the duration of their studies, from the time the first child went to university, till the last finished her degree, we had meat for that Sunday table, and when they finished their studies, the flow of meat stopped! Wonderful provision! Their friends must have thought that we were well heeled for they had good helpings of roast beef and Yorkshire pudding with all the trappings every Sunday for all those years. Mary did us proud, producing wonderful meals, and we so enjoyed the animated crack around that table as their scintillating conversation sent us into peels of laughter again and again.

When we left the Faith Mission College, we needed to step into the realm of computers. Our son took us to a computer firm and priced everything that we would need to begin this venture. It came to £1,430. A few days later the college gave us a great send-off meal and handed us a cheque from all the Faith Mission workers and friends. It was exactly £1,430!

We went for a holiday to Lewis. We were away for three weeks and when I checked, I found that it had cost £450. I had preached a few times and received honorariums. Here and there we had received small gifts, but they all added up to £450!

The dentist's bill was £85. Mary visited a lady who had spiritual need, and who, when she left, handed her an envelope which contained £80.

Our car repairs cost just over £450. On the very day that we were given this news, we received two letters, one from Australia and another from someone in Scotland. The one contained £395 and the other £50, a total of £445. The Lord had prompted people in different parts of the globe to give practical support and had arranged that the cheques should arrive together on the day that we needed them with almost the exact amount required.

In our new home in Broxburn, after our retirement, we had three crises where several things happened almost simultaneously. The drains were blocked and had to be cleared, the electricity box needed to be replaced, and there was yet another issue, each of which cost about £300. Amazingly, from different parts of the country, three cheques arrived each of about £300 the very week that we received the bills!

When we were living on the north side of the city near to the old college, our non-church-going neighbours were throwing out their large deepfreeze. They offered it to us and it has been working well for twenty years!

A WEDDING TO REMEMBER

Let me tell briefly the story of Christine's wedding. Weddings cost! Christine came in one day in tears having seen the price of wedding dresses and knowing that we would not be able to meet the cost of the dresses and the reception. Her wedding would be a terrible failure! I drew her to me and said, 'My darling, God has never let us down. We'll trust God!'

On the very day that Christine was so upset, a cheque for £1,000 arrived in the post. That was a good start! Paul Crowe, a Faith Mission worker, formerly a chef, said to me, 'Mr Peckham, I'll give you a week and do the whole reception—and please, no payment for me.'

The college gave us permission to use the tent-covered quadrangle which holds a congregation of about 450. This meant that we would not have to pay for a venue! Paul purchased foodstuffs on the college account at a reduced rate, and tables were set up for the reception.

Christine was involved in her demanding dissertation in the final year of her B.Sc. (Hons.), together with a number of other pressing issues. And now on top of it all came the wedding. If she had not been organized, it would have been a disaster. I said to Philip, her husband to be, 'Christine is organized, you know.'

'Organized?' he exclaimed. 'We can invade Europe!'

Christine found the desired silk fabric for her dress on a sale at half price. The dress was made for a mere £150. Her friend Nicola, who was studying art, made a magnificent tiara with their special materials for £10. Other items were purchased at amazingly low prices at just the time that the prices were lowered. A friend in South Africa made 150 beautiful little bags for favours and they were filled with goodies for the guests. Flowers in the church and at the reception were given at cost price with free labour. One thing after another was acquired at extremely low prices. Even the jeweller reduced the price of the rings by 13%. There were a series of remarkable coincidences—or shall we call them answers to prayer—just little miracles!

When we were in America, folk from a church where we were ministering took us to an outfitter and fitted both Mary and me with wedding garments.

There was a great deal of initiative, resourcefulness and sheer hard work with the wonderful hand of the Lord working with us.

Money came from most unexpected sources. Gifts of different amounts came from all over—£100 here and £150 there. A former worker, long retired, gave a tea-set and £100 that she had carefully put aside.

There were about 180 guests at the reception and Paul presented a wonderful meal for about £5.50 per head. At the end, Philip's grandfather gratefully gave Paul £100—something he could not refuse—a beautiful touch.

We bowed in gratitude to the One who had so marvellously provided. He did not let us down nor put us to shame. His name is Jehovah-jireh—the LORD will provide!

The provisions for Heather's wedding were not as dramatic as this first one, for Heather had been teaching for a while before her marriage and there was not the frantic rush at the end of the academic year as had been the case at Christine's wedding. Nevertheless, there were such beautiful touches of the Lord's good hand upon the whole event. It too was a wonderful occasion and we praise the Lord for his gracious hand upon us, providing for the weddings of both our girls.

I could go on and on telling story after wonderful story of God's marvellous provision. When we did not need money, none came, yet when we needed it, amazingly and uncannily, it arrived! Of course, there were the testing times when we were brought again to recognize our dependence on God for our very lives.

RETIREMENT ACCOMMODATION

The acquisition of our house is another remarkable story. The savings which we had brought to the UK from South Africa had been used up. We were not in the public eye, being at the college behind four walls, and consequently did not receive many financial gifts. What were we to do about a home in the future? One night after a convention service in Edinburgh, we had some folk around for tea. One man said, 'I just thank the Lord that I have been able to give £162,000 to the work of the Lord this year.'

I called across the room, 'You can lend us some to start us off.'

'How much do you want?' he called out.

'Ten thousand pounds,' I replied. It was just a big joke and everybody laughed. After the tea he came to me and said, 'Do you really want some money?'

'Yes,' I said, 'we are going towards retirement with nothing.'

'I'll send you £10,000,' he said, 'to be paid back without interest whenever you can.'

We bought a flat in central Edinburgh, placed university students in it, and they paid off the mortgage. We paid him back as we could and after a few years had paid back £2,000. He never sent receipts and apart from ourselves no-one knew about this transaction. He was diagnosed with leukaemia and we went to see him one day as we were passing that way. He spoke openly about going to heaven, so I said to him, 'If you die, your estate will require the monies which you lent us.'

'No, they won't,' he said. Some time later he died. The minister was taken ill at the last moment before the funeral. The phone rang as we were going to the funeral from the house of friends who lived near the church, and I was asked to take the funeral service. I later wrote to his millionaire children explaining everything and telling them that we owed them £8,000. We would sell the flat to get the money to pay them as soon as they required us to do so. Six weeks later we received a letter from them to say that they had discussed the matter with their lawyers and had decided to waive the amount. We owed them nothing. The flat was now ours. For the next four years we gained from the rental, and eventually when we sold it, just before we retired, we received more than twice as much as we had paid for it.

We were going everywhere preaching the gospel and the time was passing. We had to leave the principal's house when I officially retired. We did look around a little to gauge the market but the Scottish parliament was just being established in Edinburgh and this had driven house prices up. They were away above our reach. I said, 'Please, Lord, you look for a house for us. We are busy in your work and have little time to search for a house.' Three months before we had to leave the principal's house, our daughter Heather said to me reproachfully, 'Dad! Have you got a house yet?'

'No,' I replied.

'Well, Dad!' stated Heather emphatically, 'this is either great faith or sheer irresponsibility!"'

I went back to a lady who had a house for sale in Broxburn, just outside of Edinburgh. 'I sold my house five days ago,' she said, 'but my sister-in-law, just around the corner, has a nice house for sale.' I went there and found a splendid detached house in a cul-de-sac, altogether suitable. We had asked the Lord for three things: a house on one level; a small garden (please, not large!); and space to store my library of 4,000 books. God wonderfully provided all three, for the double garage was converted into a library.

In fact when we met a friend and told him about the double garage which we wanted to convert to a library and a cassette/CD office, he simply said, 'That sounds like a good project. I'll pick up the bill for that.' I was astounded and thrilled at how God provided. He sent £3,000 and this was a great boost to getting it done. God went before us and stepped into the situation.

I retired in June, 2001, and we settled the deal with the lady in Broxburn, and then moved into the house with no debt or mortgage at all! Amazing! Just a few years ago we had nothing, and now we had a house, completely paid for with no mortgage. For months afterwards we would gaze around and say to each other, 'This is our house!' God had wonderfully provided!

Months before we had to leave the college property, I had drawn on paper, as accurately to scale as I could, what I thought we would need as a house, and had laid it before the Lord. Some time after we had moved into the house in Broxburn, I came upon this sketch and was amazed to find that it was almost the same as the actual house we had now purchased! We have a wonderful Lord.

'Retired,' did I say? 'Re-tyred, more like it!' Our home simply became a base for further ministry, and we have been privileged still to be in the service of the Lord as we seek to serve him in many places in this and other countries. From here I am still writing books and praying that God will continue to use us as we give ourselves to him for time and eternity.

In the midst of all this I have realized all along the way, and now still realize only too well, that, having done all, I am an unprofitable servant. In fact, I have wept at times at the realization that I could have done so much more, that I could have been so much more dedicated, that I could have handled things better, that I made a mess here and there. I have known so much of the mercy of God, and so little of the power of God. How much more I could have been at his disposal; how much more he could have poured himself through me, how much more I could have glorified him, how much more of his power and glory I could have experienced. Mary has had to dig me out of a dark hole on several occasions when I considered myself hopelessly inadequate for the task and incapable of fulfilling God's desires. Yet he has had mercy on me and has helped, strengthened, assisted and guided and by his grace used me in some very small measure, to bring glory to his wonderful Name! My life is his, now and for ever!

OUR CHILDREN

Before they were even conceived, we gave to the Lord any children who might be born to this marriage, and prayed for them and for their prospective partners. They have been carried in prayer all along the way. God has been with them in a wonderful way and they are all serving the Lord, for which we are very grateful! All their spouses come from wonderful Christian homes and this, too, is as source of joy and gratitude.

Christine, an occupational therapist, was married first. Her husband is Philip Jensen, an architect turned businessman/manager for Procter and

Gamble. He approached me very carefully and asked: 'May I have your daughter's hand, and the rest of her as well, in marriage?'

I slowly replied: 'I have never been asked such a question, so I'll have to think about it for a few weeks!' We had a good laugh, and of course he was so welcome in our family. They were involved from the beginning in church work, and have been leading student ministries particularly in their Newcastle church. They are both, at the moment, in the postgraduate divinity course at Talbot Seminary, Biola University, Los Angeles, and have two small children, Samuel and Eve.

Heather, a primary school teacher, married next. Dr Adrian Holdsworth is a laser scientist. Both were well experienced in areas of church leadership. He left his research work to enter the Faith Mission College with Heather for the two years. They worked in the Faith Mission for a year before going to Moody Bible Institute, Chicago, where they are both studying divinity at postgraduate level.

Colin married Norma Staig, a physiotherapist, from Dalkeith, near Edinburgh. He equipped himself with a B.Mus.(Hons). and a B.Th., and founded an organization called Origin which consists of a choir of about a hundred and an orchestra of about forty-five, all of which he conducts. Origin hires the largest halls which are filled again and again, and where the gospel is preached after the gospel concert or Christian praise. He and Norma moved to Cape Town, South Africa, where they are establishing Origin there. To put bread on the table he is working in the world of IT—computers.

They are all serving the Lord and we are thrilled to have them as our children. They are very precious and we pray that God will continue to bless and guide them all the way home to glory. They are carrying the flame into the next generation and we just give thanks to the Lord.

Praise the Lord indeed! To him be all the glory!

Other books by Colin Peckham

The Authority of the Bible—Christian Focus Publications, ISBN 1-85792-436-3

Exploring the Bible: Joshua—A devotional commentary, Day One Publications, ISBN 978-1-84625-093-4

Great Gospel Words—Day One Publications, ISBN 978-1-84625-138-2

Heritage of Revival—Faith Mission, ISBN 0-950-8058-15

Resisting Temptation—Christian Focus Publications, ISBN 1-85792-247-6

Scattered pearls (poetry)—privately published, ISBN 0-620-06026-3

Souls for Christ—(ca.1975)

Sounds from Heaven—The 1949 Lewis revival, Christian Focus Publications, ISBN 987-1-85792-953-9

When God guides—(ca. 1975)

Youth Challenged—ed, (ca. 1975)

When God came down—The North Uist revival, by John Ferguson (with foreword and contributions from Colin N Peckham and others), Lewis Recordings, ISBN 0-951-4599-7-X

Photo gallery

Doris Annie Peckham,
Colin's mother

Auntie Mackie, who
married Bertie Peckham

AEB Onrus River convention
near Cape Town

**Preaching at Beulah Gardens,
near Madras, India**

**Faith Mission staff and students at
the Bangor convention, 1986**

Mary and Colin in recent years